Your

and S   ngs

2003–04

Your Taxes and Savings 2003–04

A GUIDE FOR OLDER PEOPLE

Paul Lewis

AGE Concern

BOOKS

Published by Age Concern England
1268 London Road
London SW16 4ER

© 2003 Age Concern England

Twenty-fifth Edition

First published 1978

Editor Ro Lyon
Production Vinnette Marshall
Designed and typeset by GreenGate Publishing Services, Tonbridge, Kent
Printed in Great Britain by Bell & Bain Ltd, Glasgow

A catalogue record for this book is available from the British Library.

ISBN 0-86242-365-1

While every effort has been made to check the accuracy of material contained in this publication, Age Concern England cannot accept any legal responsibility for the results of investments made by readers. Inclusion in this book does not constitute a recommendation by Age Concern England for any particular product, company, service or publication.

The publishers would like to thank John Andrews of the Low Income Research Group for his suggestions and help in checking this book.

CONTENTS

ABOUT THE AUTHOR

Paul Lewis is a freelance financial journalist who writes widely on tax, benefits, and personal finance. His work appears regularly in *The Daily Telegraph*, *Saga Magazine* and *Reader's Digest*. Paul also presents *Money Box* on BBC Radio 4.

INTRODUCTION

For most people in the UK, retirement is longer and healthier at the start of the 21st century than it has ever been. On average we can now expect 20 to 30 years of life after we stop work. Of course, that is good news in many ways. But it does mean that we have to be sure that the financial decisions we make are sensible and that our money will stretch to cover that very long period of our lives.

Ideally, we should have been planning since our 30s or even earlier. Most of us, of course, did not. However, even if you are on the threshold of retirement – or have already retired – there are still things you can do to improve your financial position and make your life more comfortable.

The first step in planning a successful journey is to know where you are starting from. That means making a thorough assessment of your current financial position: your outgoings, your income and your assets.

Your outgoings

The first step is to work out the level of income you need in order to sustain a comfortable standard of living in retirement. Try and make allowance for all your likely expenditure during the course of a year. Remember that if you get untaxed income, you may have to pay tax on it later in the year.

If you have not yet retired, you may find it easier to list your current expenditure, then make an estimate of how it is likely to change once you retire. Some costs will go down – for example, you will no longer have to pay to travel to your job, for work clothes, or for lunch or refreshments on your journey.

On the other hand, some costs are likely to go up. You will be spending more time at home so fuel bills may rise, you may use your car more, if you have one, and you may spend more on hobbies or going out. Your food bills may rise and you may have to start buying things such as newspapers and pay for daytime phone calls which you got free at work.

Your income

The other side of the equation is, of course, your income, which is likely to change more than your expenditure. For most people in work, wages or self-employed earnings are their only significant source of income. Once you retire, however, income tends to come from a variety of sources.

Of course, you may still work even though you have retired. Many people do part-time or even full-time work after they 'retire' from their main job. With longer life and better health, working is a good way to boost income in retirement.

If you paid full National Insurance contributions while you worked – and everyone except the very low paid and some married women do so – you will currently get the State Pension at 65 if you are a man or 60 if you are a woman. (There is more about the State Pension on pages 138–139.)

Many people in work pay into an occupational pension scheme with their job. Your last employer should let you know what you can expect from that pension scheme. If you have done a number of jobs it is possible that you have an entitlement to a variety of pensions. If you have lost track of any occupational pensions, the Pension Schemes Registry (address on page 169) may be able to help. It has details of 200,000 pension schemes and can tell you how to make contact with any past scheme you have may have lost touch with.

In addition you may have paid into a personal pension or into an additional voluntary contribution scheme. You should have the paperwork for these yourself. Make sure you check all these sources when you retire. If you have paid into a personal pension, you will be responsible for turning the pension fund you have built up into a pension. If the fund is less than £250,000 it is normal to buy an annuity – at age 75 you have to do that anyway. You can keep 25 per cent of your fund as a tax-free lump sum. So you have to decide what to do with that too. The company where your pension was saved up is probably not the best company to buy the annuity from. There is more advice on annuities and the choices you have to make on page 146.

State benefits

It is important to check that you are receiving all the State benefits you may be entitled to. You may, for example, qualify for help with your rent or Council Tax through Housing Benefit or Council Tax Benefit. They are means-tested and you should contact your local council for more details. Remember that if you live alone you can get your Council Tax reduced by 25 per cent anyway regardless of your income. If your income is low, and your savings no more than £12,000, you may get extra weekly money through Income Support (called Minimum Income Guarantee if you are 60 or more). From October 2003 Minimum Income Guarantee will be replaced by Pension Credit and the £12,000 limit on savings will be scrapped. Five million pensioners will be better off. So see if you can claim.

If you are unemployed, under pension age and actively seeking work, you should register for Jobseeker's Allowance at the local Jobcentre Plus office. More information about JSA is provided on page 159.

You can get advice at a Citizens Advice Bureau or your local social security office. A new Pension Service is being launched by the Department for Work and Pensions to deal with all enquiries from people over 60. National sources of help are listed in the Age Concern Books annual publication *Your Rights* (see page 174), which also covers in detail the various State benefits available for many different situations, or you can get a copy of the leaflet RM1 *Retirement* from your local social security office.

Your assets

As part of your financial review, you should also make a list of all your assets. These are the things you own which could possibly be used to boost your income or provide you with a lump sum in the future. The list should include your money or savings, as well as any money you may have a right to in the future, such as a pension fund, an endowment policy or even inheritance. Write down other assets too, such as your home and car as well as any jewellery or valuables. It is probably a good idea to get all the money at your disposal down in a single list. You may find it helpful to analyse each item on the list according to the income it produces or the capital it would raise if sold.

Your skills and abilities are also part of your assets and can be used to make money. Write down the things you are good at or have a particular skill or expertise in.

Your debts

In retirement you will have less income and should try to cut down on debt. There is no point in saving money at 3 per cent and borrowing it at 10 per cent or more. So write down all your debts and see how – and how quickly – you can get rid of them. There is more information on managing debt on pages 156–157.

Your financial strategy

Once you have a clear idea of your current financial position, you can start to think seriously about your future financial goals.

Increasing your income

If your current income falls short of your outgoings, you must rectify the situation. There are a number of ways in which you may be able to boost your retirement income. For example:

- If you are currently still in work, it may not be too late to boost your pension (see pages 138–148 for more information).
- If you are already retired and struggling to make ends meet, you should find out whether you are entitled to any State benefits on top of the State Pension (see page x).
- It may be possible to raise income from your home. You may be able to take in a lodger, for example, or raise money on it directly (see pages 151–154).
- You could consider taking a part-time, or even a full-time, job or perhaps become self-employed using the skills you wrote down earlier (the Age Concern Books publication *Changing*

Direction – see page 174 – will give you plenty of ideas to think about).

- You may be able to earn more money by reorganising your savings and investments. Chapter 2 explains most common types of savings and investment schemes. The tips will help everyone, not only those who are struggling to make ends meet. Almost all of us can make our money work a bit harder and earn a bit more without taking any risk with it.

Financial aims

Whatever your financial circumstances, you should review your savings and investments from time to time. In order to do this, it is important that you are clear about your financial aims:

- Is income your main priority or do you need to build up your capital for a particular purchase, or for possible future needs?
- Are you prepared to take any risk with your money? Chapter 2 explains the difference between saving and investing. Financial advisers will tell you that the more risk you take with your money, the better the return you can expect. But they often forget to tell you that 'risk' means you may lose some or all of it. We are all familiar with the financial health warning that accompanies advertisements for share-based investments: 'The value of investments may fall as well as rise.' Over the last few years many people have found that the value of investments can fall as well as plummet. Risk means just what it says – you *may* get a better return but you *may* lose your capital.
- Remember too that money loses value every day as inflation eats away at what it will buy. If you put it in a bank or building society and leave it for 20 years it may be worth much less at the end of that process. With inflation at 2.5 per cent, the value of money halves every 28 years.
- Do you need access to your money? If you can afford to tie your money up for several years, you may be able to secure a better return.

- Are you concerned that your family should benefit from your money after your death? If not, then your objective is to use it all up before you die. If you are, then you may want to invest with one eye on Inheritance Tax planning. Either way, your attitude to leaving money behind will affect your investment choices.
- What rate of tax do you pay? Tax-free income is of more value to higher-rate taxpayers as they save more tax. Some investments are better for non-taxpayers. You must always make sure that the right amount of tax is taken off your money.
- Do you want your investments to take account of your ethical concerns? It is not just vegetarians and pacifists who are concerned about the companies they are lending their money to. There is a growing ethical investment movement with very broad ethical and environmental concerns.

Once you have established what your financial aims are, the next step is to consider whether your current investments do the job. You may want to move some of your money around as a result of this exercise. Whatever strategy you adopt, always make sure that you have some easy-access cash for emergencies. The usefulness of cash machines should not be given up for a trifling bit of extra interest.

Your Taxes

No-one likes paying tax. Yet every year we pay hundreds of millions of pounds more than we should. One reason is that the tax system is very complicated. The other is that most people know very little about it and most of us do not find working out our tax very interesting. This part of the book will help you make sure that you don't pay more tax than you should.

Tax is not just for the rich. Most people over 65 pay tax if their income is more than £127 a week. If you are under 65, you normally pay tax on anything over £89 a week. Even if your income is less than that, tax is automatically deducted from your savings without your even knowing about it. You have to take action to get it back.

Information in this book mainly covers the tax year 6 April 2003 to 5 April 2004 and includes the changes announced in the April 2003 Budget. However, if you are completing a tax return for 2002–2003 – which will normally have arrived in April 2003 – you will need to know last year's figures too. A summary of rates and allowances for both years is given at the end of this section on page 61.

THE TAX SYSTEM

There are four main taxes that affect individuals:

- Income Tax – around half of the people aged over 60 pay
  Income Tax. It is due on your income from pensions,
  interest earned on savings, some social security benefits, or,
  of course, on earnings. We explain tax allowances, the rates
  of tax, and help you to see how much tax you should pay –
  and if you can claim a rebate. We also look at self-
  assessment, which can apply to people who are self-
  employed, have untaxed income from savings, pay higher-
  rate tax or sometimes just have an income above £18,300.
- National Insurance contributions (pages 42–43) – must be
  paid by almost everyone under pension age who is
  employed or self-employed.
- Capital Gains Tax (pages 53–56) – very few people pay
  CGT each year, but it can sneak up on you. It is a tax on
  the growth in value of an asset and is normally due when
  you get rid of it – either by selling it or giving it away. It can
  also apply if you get a sudden windfall from an insurance
  company when it converts from a society to a company.
- Inheritance Tax (pages 57–59) – is a tax on the money and
  assets you leave when you die. Very few people have to pay
  IHT but, like CGT, it can take people with fairly modest
  means by surprise. We explain how to reduce the risk of
  your relatives losing out when you die. Sometimes, gifts you
  made in the seven years before you die can be taxed as well.

The Inland Revenue is the government department responsible
for these four taxes and pages 34–36 give information about
dealing with the Inland Revenue. On page 60 there is
information about Stamp Duty, due when you buy a home
worth more than £60,000.

This book does not deal with Council Tax. For information
about Council Tax, see Age Concern Factsheet 21 *The Council
Tax and older people* (details of how to obtain Age Concern
factsheets are given on page 171).

INCOME TAX

Income Tax is assessed over the 'tax year' which, for historical reasons, runs from 6 April to the following 5 April. This book covers the rules that apply for the year 6 April 2003 to 5 April 2004.

The principle behind Income Tax is simple. You are allowed a certain amount of income each year without paying tax on it at all. The rest of your income is taxed, and the bigger your income the higher the rate of tax you pay on it. However, the detailed way the system works is now very complicated and sometimes leaves even experts scratching their heads. This section explains the rules as simply and clearly as possible and should help you work out if you should pay any tax and, if so, how much.

Pages 4–14 give details about which parts of your income are tax-free and how different types of income are taxed.

Pages 15–19 explain about tax allowances (ie the amounts of income you can have before tax is due). The rates of tax in 2003–2004 are:

Income above your tax allowances	Rate of tax
Up to £1,960	Starting rate – 10 per cent
£1,961–£30,500	Basic rate – 20 per cent on interest, 10 per cent on dividends, 22 per cent on everything else
Over £30,500	Higher rate – 40 per cent

There is information to help you understand tax forms and details about the system of self-assessment, rebates, underpayments and dealing with problems and pages 45–52 explain how to check your tax bill, and examples are included.

YOUR INCOME

Most income is taxable – that means if you have too much of it, you will have to pay tax. However some income is not taxable however much money you have.

Taxable income

Taxable income includes:

- wages and earnings;
- the State Pension and all other pensions including company and personal pensions; and
- some social security benefits such as Bereavement Allowance, Carer's Allowance, and Statutory Sick Pay.

Incapacity Benefit is a bit more complicated. If you claimed it for the first time after 12 April 1995 and you have received it for at least 28 weeks, then it is taxable. Otherwise it is not.

The interest on savings and investments, and the rent you receive from property you own, are normally taxable but there are some exceptions which are listed below.

Non-taxable income

Some types of income are not taxable. That means they are ignored completely when your Income Tax is calculated. Income that is not taxable includes:

- all social security benefits that depend on your income, such as Council Tax Benefit, Housing Benefit, Income Support (normally called Minimum Income Guarantee for people over 60), Pension Credit (from October 2003); and

Money-saving tip: Probably a million people aged over 60 do not claim the help they could get with their Council Tax, their rent or their income in general. Hundreds of millions of pounds is going unclaimed. Also, five million pensioners will be able to

claim Pension Credit from October 2003. Ask for advice at your local Age Concern or Citizen's Advice Bureau.

- any Child Tax Credit or Working Tax Credit.

Money-saving tip: Tax credits are not well understood but if you have low pay or a dependant child you may be able to claim.

- Most benefits paid on account of a disability or illness are also tax-free. These include Attendance Allowance, Disability Living Allowance (care and mobility components), Industrial Injuries Benefit, War Disablement Pension, War Widow's Pension, other disablement pensions from the police, fire brigade, merchant navy, and Severe Disablement Allowance. Incapacity Benefit is tax-free for the first six months you receive it (and if you claimed it before 13 April 1995, and have claimed it continuously since, it is always tax-free).

- The £10 Christmas Bonus and the £200 or £300 Winter Fuel Payment for people aged 60 or more are tax-free, as is the £2,000 Bereavement Payment which a husband or wife may get when their partner dies. Child Benefit is also tax-free. The one-off £10,000 payment to people who were Prisoners of War of the Japanese is tax-free and so are pension annuities paid by Austria and Germany to the victims of Nazi persecution.

- Some investment income is tax-free. The gains on National Savings certificates and the interest from a National Savings ordinary account are free of tax. Interest earned on an Individual Savings Account (ISA) is tax-free (see pages 110–111). You can no longer buy a TESSA or a PEP but if you still have one then the income or gains on it will always be tax-free.

Tax-saving tip: If you do not pay tax there is often not much point in putting your money in a non-taxable savings product.

- If you rent out a room in your home, up to £4,250 rent in the year is tax-free. You can find out more in the Inland Revenue leaflet IR 87 *Letting and your home*.
- Prizes from gambling are normally free of all tax – that includes winnings on premium bonds, football pools, racing, and Lotto, the National Lottery. However, if you make your living from gambling then the income can be taxable.
- Gifts, even gifts of money you receive regularly, are free of tax. But if you are given money in exchange for doing work or providing a service then that is counted as earnings and is taxable.
- Maintenance payments made to a divorced or separated spouse, or to the children, are tax-free.

Leaving your job

If you are made redundant, the first £30,000 of any redundancy payment is tax-free and the rest is taxable. However, if you are entitled to a leaving payment under your contract of employment, then the whole of it will be taxed before you receive it. The Inland Revenue may challenge the exemption on redundancy money if it considers that your redundancy was not genuine; for example if it was early retirement.

Tax-saving tip – if the Inland Revenue questions the tax-free status of a redundancy payment, challenge it. Get advice as the Revenue does make mistakes.

If you get a lump sum for an injury or disability which prevents you from continuing to work, it should be tax-free, as should be a payment made when you leave a job where you mainly worked abroad.

If you leave a job after less than two years, you may get a refund of the contributions you have paid into your employer's pension scheme. Tax at 20 per cent is usually deducted from the refund before it is paid to you.

How income is taxed

Earnings, occupational pensions and personal pensions

Tax on your earnings and on any pensions you get from an employer's pension scheme or a personal pension plan is collected though a system known as Pay As You Earn (PAYE). If you are self-employed, your profits will be taxed through the self-assessment system which is described on pages 25–30, but your pension will normally still be taxed through PAYE. The tax is deducted by your employer or the pension scheme or annuity provider before you see the money. They work out the tax due using a tax code provided by the Inland Revenue. Tax codes are just a way of collecting tax, not of assessing it, and the tax deducted is always approximate. So it is very important that you check how much tax you have paid in the tax year and if it is correct. There is more on tax codes and how they can go wrong on pages 20–24.

If you change jobs, the employer you leave should give you a form called a P45, which shows your tax code. Give it to your new employer so that they can deduct the correct amount of tax. Until your employer has your P45 your earnings will normally be taxed on what is called an emergency code. That may mean you pay too much tax.

In some circumstances you will start a job and not have a P45. That might happen if you retired from a job, got an occupational pension and then took up a new job. If you do not have a P45, your new employer should ask you to sign form P46 and give you form P15 (allowances claim) so that the right PAYE code can be obtained for taxing your earnings.

If you have more than one income taxed under PAYE – for example, two occupational pensions or a pension and a job – then the tax code is applied to the bigger source of income. The other income will normally be taxed in full at the basic rate. So you will have 22 per cent deducted from all of it before you are paid.

If you have bought an annuity at the end of a personal pension plan or a stakeholder pension, then tax is deducted under PAYE. However, if you started your pension plan before personal pension plans started on 1 July 1988, then it is called a 'retirement annuity contract' (or a Section 226 pension) and is normally paid to you with 22 per cent tax deducted before you receive it.

There is another sort of annuity called a 'purchased life annuity'. These are not bought as part of a retirement plan but are simply an investment. Part of the money you get is simply a return of the capital sum you paid for the annuity and this is not taxed. The rest represents the investment income earned by the capital and is taxed at 20 per cent. There is more information about annuities as investments on pages 112–113.

With a Section 226 pension or a purchased life annuity the tax deducted may not be right. If you pay higher-rate tax, you will have to pay more tax through your self-assessment form. If you are only due to pay tax at the lower rate or no tax at all, you can claim back the overpaid tax. If you are due to pay no tax, then you can have the income on a pension annuity paid gross if you apply on form R89 (which you can get from your local tax office or from the annuity provider).

Tax-saving tip: If you have an annuity, check that the correct tax has been deducted.

The State Pension and benefits

The State Pension is taxable but it is paid without tax being deducted. That applies whether it is paid in cash through the Post Office or directly into your bank account (the Government wants almost all pensions to be paid into a bank or post office account by 2005). The tax on it is collected from your earnings or other pension by changing your tax code. So it may seem, for example, that you are being taxed heavily on your occupational pension, but that is because you are having tax deducted from your occupational pension to pay the tax due on your State Pension.

If you only have the State Pension it is unlikely that you will have to pay any tax. However, some people (especially women under 65) can have a State Pension, including the State Earnings-Related Pension Scheme (SERPS) or its replacement the State Second Pension (S2P), which is big enough by itself for tax to be due on it. If you have no other pension or earnings then the tax will have to be paid through the self-assessment scheme. There is more information on self-assessment on pages 25–30.

The State Pension paid to a married woman aged 60 or more, whether based on her own contributions or her husband's, counts as her income. However, if a married man gets extra State Pension for his wife who is under pension age, then that it is taxed as part of his income.

Example

Paul Davies is 65 and his wife Mary is 59 and does not work. Because Mary is under 60, Paul claims an extra £46.35 on his pension for her. It is called an Adult Dependency Increase. This extra pension is taxed as his income. However, once Mary reaches 60, this extra pension stops and Mary can claim a married woman's pension of £46.35 on Paul's National Insurance contributions. It is paid to her and is counted as her income when tax is worked out.

Similar rules apply in the rare cases where a woman gets an Adult Dependency Increase for her husband.

Money-saving tip: Many married women have paid some full contributions in the past before they were married. That can entitle them to a pension in their own right which they can claim at 60. If they worked between 1961 and 1975 they will also have earned some graduated retirement benefit. Contact your local social security office to make sure that the Department for Work and Pensions (DWP) knows about all your previous jobs and addresses so it can give you the correct pension.

Other taxable social security benefits, such as Bereavement Allowance or Incapacity Benefit (in some circumstances), may be less than your tax allowances and so no tax is in fact due. However, if you are liable for Income Tax, it will be collected by adjusting your tax code if you have another source of income such as an occupational pension; otherwise, it can be deducted at source so the benefit will be paid to you net of Income Tax.

If you have a pension from abroad, it will be paid without tax being deducted. There is a special concession on most pensions paid from abroad which means that only 90 per cent of the amount is taxable. If you get a pension from abroad, it is likely you will be sent a self-assessment form. Your tax office or tax enquiry centre can tell you more about tax on pensions or other income from abroad. Alternatively, the tax on the pension may be collected by adjusting your tax code.

Tax-saving tip: If you get a pension from abroad, make sure that the amount of tax you pay at the end of the year is correct – mistakes are common.

Savings income

Interest paid on savings or investments is taxed in two different ways. Some interest is paid 'gross' – ie, without tax being deducted first. If you pay tax, you will have to pay the tax on it later. However, most interest and investment income is paid with the tax already deducted. Tax on dividends paid on shares is taxed in a peculiar way which is explained on page 25. Of course, some interest is tax-free – that is listed above on pages 4–6.

Interest paid gross

Some sorts of interest are paid gross. Interest from taxable National Savings products is always paid gross. The interest paid on Government stock, also called 'gilts', is paid gross unless you specifically ask for it to be paid net of tax. If you have money invested in a bank or building society outside the UK, that will normally be paid gross too. If your total income is too low to pay tax, then you will not have to worry about paying tax on income paid gross. But if you have to pay tax, this will be done in one of two ways. If you have earnings paid through PAYE and your interest received gross totals less than £2,500, the tax on it can be collected through your PAYE code. If not, you will be sent a self-assessment tax form to account for the tax due (see pages 25–30).

Tax on interest

The basic rate of tax for income from savings is 20 per cent. This rate applies to almost all types of income from savings, including interest on bank and building society accounts, taxable National Savings products and annuities that you purchase as an investment (called purchased life annuities), but not retirement annuities that you have to buy with a pension fund, which are taxed at the same rate as earnings.

In April 1999 a 10 per cent starting tax rate was introduced. This tax year, 2003–2004, the 10 per cent starting rate covers the first £1,960 of taxable income, including income from savings.

If your income is high – above around £35,115 in the year – you will normally have to pay higher-rate tax, which is 40 per cent, on your savings income.

Joint savings of husbands and wives

If a husband and wife have savings or investments in their joint names, any income will normally be split equally for tax purposes. However, if you actually own the asset unequally you may be able to make a joint declaration setting out how it is owned and each of you will be taxed on your actual share of the income. Ask at your tax office for further information.

Tax-saving tip: A couple may be able to save tax by transferring savings to the partner who pays no tax or tax at a lower rate (see pages 50–52). If you have a joint account with a partner who pays no tax, only half the interest is payable.

Bank and building society accounts

Interest paid on money you have in a bank or building society account has 20 per cent tax deducted from it automatically. The basic rate of tax on savings income is 20 per cent. Even if you are not liable to pay tax, or only to pay it at the lower, 10 per cent rate, you will have the full 20 per cent deducted automatically.

Tax-saving tip: check your bank and building society accounts to see how much tax has been deducted. If too much has been taken off, you can get it back for up to six tax years.

If your income is too low to pay tax, then you can apply for the interest to be paid gross, without tax being deducted. So if you expect your total gross income for the year to be less than your tax allowances, apply to have the interest paid gross by completing form R85, which is available from your bank or building society or from a tax office. You will need to fill in a separate form for each account you have. If you have a joint account, then any of the account holders who is a non-taxpayer can fill in the form. For example, if the husband pays tax and the wife does not, then half the interest can be paid tax free.

If you are a non-taxpayer but do not apply for bank or building society interest to be paid gross, or you are liable to pay tax on some but not all of your interest, or you are only liable for tax at the 10 per cent rate, you can apply for a refund of any tax overpaid. You can also make an application if you have overpaid tax in the last six years, back to the year 1997–1998. You can reclaim any overpaid tax on interest after the tax year ends or once the amount owed reaches £50. (See pages 31–32 for further information about claiming a tax rebate.)

If you are a basic-rate taxpayer, income paid with tax deducted must be taken into account when calculating your total income to determine whether you are entitled to the higher allowances for people aged 65 or over (see page 15). The amount you receive is 'grossed up' in order to check what your total gross income is. To take into account the tax already deducted, every £80 of net interest you receive is treated by the tax office as

£100 gross income. So to 'gross up' your net savings income, divide by 4 and multiply by 5.

Example

Mark Heaney is 65 and retired from work in March 2003. His income for the year from State and occupational pensions totals £6,110. As he is 65, his tax allowance is £6,610. He also gets interest from a bank account, which he expects to be £456 this year. So he thinks his total income is £6,566, still below his tax allowance. However, he has forgotten to gross up his additional income from interest. If he divides it by 4 and multiplies by 5 he gets £570 which takes his total income up to £6,680. So he cannot apply to get his interest paid gross.

Dividend income

If you own shares, you will normally be paid a dividend once or twice a year. These dividends are taxed in a peculiar way. You will be sent the money net of tax. However, the tax on dividends is only 10 per cent. So if your dividend is £100, you will be sent £90 (£100 minus £10) and the document that accompanies the cheque will also show what is called a 'tax credit' of £10, showing you have paid £10 tax. If your income is not high enough to pay tax you cannot claim back this £10. Take care of this document as you will need to keep it as part of your tax records. You will also need the figures to work out your tax liability.

If you have to pay higher-rate tax, then you will have to pay extra tax on the dividend you have received in the tax year. Your gross dividend income will be taxed at the rate of 32.5 per cent. As you have already paid 10 per cent, you will owe a further 22.5 per cent on the gross dividend, which is 25 per cent of the net dividend. You can work out the gross amount of the dividend by adding up the amount you got and the tax credit. Even if you do not pay higher-rate tax you will need to be able to work out the grossed-up amount to see if you are entitled to the higher tax allowances for people aged 65 or more.

The tax credit was reduced from 20 per cent to 10 per cent in April 1999. Before April 1999 tax credits could be repaid to non-taxpayers or those who had not used up all their allowances – but now they cannot. However, you can still claim for two tax years before the rules changed (the years 1997–1998 to 1998–1999) if you have not already done so.

Unit trusts and OEICs

The income from unit trusts or open-ended investment companies (OEICs) (see pages 105–106) can be paid either as interest or as dividends. If it is paid as interest – often called an 'interest distribution' – it is treated like interest on money in a bank or building society. If it is paid as a dividend, it is taxed like dividends.

Other investment income

If you have purchased an annuity as an investment, rather than as part of a pension plan, only part of the money you get each month is treated as income – the rest is treated as a return of your capital. The income part is normally paid with 20 per cent tax automatically deducted. If your income is below your tax allowances, or you are only due to pay tax at the 10 per cent rate, you can claim back some tax. If you are due to pay tax at the higher rate, then you will have to pay extra tax on this income.

The Inland Revenue is keen to help people claim back tax they may have overpaid on savings and investments. You can ring the Taxback Helpline on 0845 077 6543. Calls are charged at local rates. There is also a useful booklet IR 110 *Bank and building society interest: A guide for savers*, which is available from tax offices or on the Inland Revenue website at www.inlandrevenue.gov.uk

---

TAX ALLOWANCES

Each year we are allowed to have a certain amount of income before we have to pay any tax on it. This is called a Personal Allowance. Blind people get an extra tax allowance. People who are married and above a certain age may also get some money deducted from their tax bill. This is often called a 'tax allowance' but it is different from the Personal Allowances and is explained on pages 17–18.

Normally, if your income is less than your allowances, you will not have to pay tax. If your income is more than your allowances, some tax will be due, although for most people it will have been taken off some of their income already.

Personal Allowance

This allowance is available to everyone – men, women, married or single – and is set at three different levels depending on your age. For 2003–2004 they are:

- £4,615 for people aged under 65 (the same as last year);
- £6,610 for people aged between 65 and 74; or
- £6,720 for people aged 75 or more.

You can claim the higher Personal Allowance for a whole tax year (6 April to 5 April) if you reach 65 or 75 at any time during the year. So, even if your 65th or 75th birthday is on 5 April 2004 you can claim the higher allowance for the whole of this tax year.

Tax-saving tip: The Inland Revenue should know your date of birth, but it does not always get it right. So if you will be 65 or 75 between 6 April 2003 and 5 April 2004 check that you get the right tax allowance this tax year.

People aged 65 or more may lose the higher allowance if their income is above a certain level. The Personal Allowance will be reduced if your total gross income is more than £18,300. For every £2 of extra income above £18,300 your allowance will be reduced by £1. The allowance is never reduced below the basic Personal Allowance of £4,615. It will be reduced to £4,615 if your income is £22,290 or more (aged 65 to 74) or £22,510 or more (aged 75 or over).

If your income is below the level of your Personal Allowance, you will not pay tax. If your income is above your Personal Allowance, then the first £1,960 is taxed at 10 per cent, the next £28,540 is taxed at the basic rate – either 22 per cent (earnings and pensions) or 20 per cent (investment income). Any income above that is taxed at 40 per cent.

However, people whose Personal Allowance is reduced because their income is over £18,300 may end up paying tax at a different rate. Income between £18,300 and around £22,300 is taxed at 30 or 33 per cent. It works like this. Each extra £2 of income is taxed at 22 per cent (or 20 per cent if it is investment income) and it reduces your allowances by £1, bringing another £1 of income liable to tax. The result is that each £2 increase in income results in tax on £3 of income. At 22 per cent that is 66p. So for each £2 of income, your tax rises by 66p or 33 per cent. If it is investment income, the tax rate is 30 per cent.

Tax-saving tip: If you are married, move assets between you to make sure that neither spouse has an income above £18,300.

The Personal Allowance is available to all individuals – married or single. If you cannot use it all, you cannot pass it on to anyone else, even a spouse. The £18,300 income limit applies separately to the income of a husband and wife.

Blind Person's Allowance

A person who is registered as blind with their local authority gets an extra tax allowance of £1,510. That means a blind person can have an extra £1,510 income in 2003–2004 before they start paying tax. A married blind person whose income is too low to use up the tax allowance can transfer it to their spouse. If both partners are blind, they can each get the £1,510 and one can transfer it to the other if they cannot use it in full.

You may be able to register as blind, even though you are not totally without sight. To be registered, you must show that your lack of sight makes it impossible to perform any work for which eyesight is essential. The Inland Revenue can also give you the allowance if you have applied to be registered as blind but this has not yet been granted. You do not, however, get the Blind Person's Allowance if you are registered with your local authority as partially sighted.

Married Couple's Allowance

Most married couples no longer get any extra tax allowance as the Married Couple's Allowance was abolished in April 2000. However, some older couples can still get it if either partner was born before 6 April 1935. So one partner has to be at least aged 68 throughout the tax year 2003–2004. The rule applies even to those who marry now. They get the full allowance in the year they marry if the marriage takes place before 6 May. If they marry on or after 6 May, the allowance is reduced by one twelfth for each whole month. In subsequent years they get the full allowance.

Despite its name, the Married Couple's Allowance is not like the personal tax allowance. It is simply a reduction in the tax that is due. It is set at two levels depending on the age of the older spouse:

Age of older spouse on 5 April 2004	Allowance	Tax deduction
68 to 74	£5,565	£556.50
75 or more	£5,635	£563.50
Minimum amount	£2,150	£215.00

The Married Couple's Allowance is normally taken off the husband's tax bill. However, a married woman can choose to have up to £1,075 of it herself if she asks (worth £107.50 off her tax) and can have £2,150 (worth £215 off her tax) with her husband's consent. The rest has to be applied to the husband's tax. Any change in the allocation of the Married Couple's Allowance must be done before the start of the tax year, so it is too late now for 2003–2004 but you could do it for 2004–2005. You should get Inland Revenue Form 18 *Transferring the Married Couple's Tax Allowance*. Once you have made the choice, it will continue to operate until you make a different choice.

A husband can also transfer the allowance if his income is too low to make use of it. This might be useful if a wife has a higher income than her husband. For example, if his income is below £6,610 and he pays no tax, then he can transfer all of the Married Couple's Allowance to his wife. This transfer can be done up to six years afterwards, so in 2003–2004 you can look back to 1997–1998 to adjust the allocation of the Married Couple's Allowance. You can either get Form 575 from a tax office, or claim on the tax return.

The allowance is reduced if the husband's income exceeds a certain amount. The calculation depends on how old he and his wife are, but normally it is reduced if his income exceeds £22,290 (aged 67 to 74) or £22,510 (aged 75 or more). Once it reaches around £30,000, the Married Couple's Allowance is reduced to £2,150 and there it stays – it cannot be reduced further. The allowance is only reduced by the husband's income even if his wife gets some of the allowance.

Widows and widowers

Tax concessions for widows were abolished in April 2000. A woman or a man who becomes widowed can continue to receive any Married Couple's Allowance that is due for that tax year. They can also receive any unused part of the Married Couple's Allowance that their spouse was entitled to in that year. The deceased person's executors should ask for this to be transferred.

Maintenance payments

Tax relief on maintenance payments was abolished from April 2000 except where at least one ex-partner was born before 6 April

1935. For them, tax relief is still available on maintenance payments to a divorced or separated spouse under a court order, a legally binding agreement or an order of the Child Support Agency. It is 10 per cent of the payment and is limited to £215 in the 2003–2004 tax year. If you receive maintenance payments under these rules, you do not have to pay tax on the payments that you receive however much they are. Voluntary payments and those paid directly to children are completely ignored by the Inland Revenue.

Child Tax Credit

If you are responsible for a child then you may get extra money called Child Tax Credit. It replaces the similarly named Children's Tax Credit but in fact it is nothing to do with tax. It is a cash amount paid direct to the main carer of the child. You may also be able to claim Child Benefit from the Inland Revenue.

For a tax credit claim form or more information contact your local tax office or ring the Tax Credit Helpline on 0845 300 3900. See also Inland Revenue leaflet *Working Tax Credit and Child Tax Credit: An introduction* WTC1 or visit the Inland Revenue website at www.taxcredits.inlandrevenue.gov.uk

---

Mortgage payments and home income plans

Interest payments on a mortgage do not qualify for tax relief. But if you have a home income plan you took out before 9 March 1999 then the first £30,000 of the mortgage that is part of the plan still has tax relief deducted at 23 per cent. The relief is part of the payment you make and does not affect your other tax calculations.

YOUR TAX CODE

A tax code is a way of collecting tax from earnings or a pension paid by an ex-employer. The Inland Revenue gives your employer or pension provider a tax code which tells them how much money to deduct from your pay or pension. Most people who get a State Pension and pay tax through PAYE are told each year what their tax code is.

Under 'Pay As You Earn' (PAYE) your annual tax allowance is divided by 12 (or 52 if you are paid weekly) so that each month (or week) you get some income free of tax, and the rest is taxed. So if your personal tax allowance was £4,615 and you had no other taxable income your employer would not tax the first £384.58 you earned each month and then would tax the rest. It all sounds very sensible and very simple. But it can get complicated.

Tax-saving tip: A tax code is simply an approximate way of collecting tax; it is not a way of assessing it. It may well result in too much tax being collected from you. Always check it and check the amount of tax you have paid at the end of the year.

The code

A tax code normally consists of a number followed by a letter. The number represents the amount of money you can have tax-free in the year with the last digit removed. So if the tax allowance is £4,615 then your code would start 461. Your employer then knows to allow you £4,619 during the year without taking any tax off. (The last figure is always a '9' to try to make sure the code system errs on your side: in other words your allowance is slightly higher than the £4,615 it should be.) That number is then followed by a letter which shows what kind of allowance you have. A common code for people under 65 is 461L – the 'L' stands for lower Personal Allowance. Quite a lot of things in tax codes are hangovers from the past.

The main letters used in codes for older people are explained below:

- **L** – you get the basic Personal Allowance for people under 65.
- **P** – you get the higher Personal Allowance for someone aged 65–74.
- **Y** – you get the higher Personal Allowance for someone aged 75 or over.
- **V** – you are a basic-rate taxpayer and get both the Personal Allowance and Married Couple's Allowance for someone aged under 75.
- **T** – is for just about anything else. For example, it may be given if your age-related Personal Allowance is reduced because your income is above the income limit. You will also get a 'T' code if you ask the tax office not to reveal to your employer or pension payer what your circumstances are.
- **K** – you have 'negative' allowances. In other words, your earnings or pension will be taxed at more than the basic rate. That happens when untaxed income, such as the State Pension or gross interest from savings, exceeds your Personal Allowances. Tax must therefore be deducted at more than the normal rate to take into account the tax that is due on your untaxed income. However, tax is never deducted at more than 50 per cent.
- **NT** – no tax is to be deducted.
- **0T** – all your earnings are to be taxed with no tax allowance.
- **BR** – tax collected at the basic rate.
- **D0** – applies only to people who pay tax at the higher rate. Their total income must be at least £35,115 in 2003–2004.

Notice of Coding

If you work or have a pension from your old job, you should get a Notice of Coding before 6 April – the start of the tax year. This will show your tax code and how it is worked out; for example, it may show your Personal Allowance and then subtract the annual amount of your State Pension. Check that the figures are right and the calculation makes sense.

Example

Irene Style is 70 and has a State Pension of £81.60 a week, which is £4,243 a year. As Irene is aged between 65 and 74, her tax allowance is £6,610. She takes her State Pension from her allowance to give £2,367 and knocks off the last digit to give 236. She checks her code and sees it is 236P. The 'P' means she gets the higher Personal Allowance for someone aged 65–74. The code means that each year she is allowed £2,369 before tax is due. So if her occupational pension is £197 a month or less, she will pay no tax on it.

If you have more than one source of income taxed through PAYE, you will have a tax code (and a Notice of Coding) for each – see page 7.

When you get a new Notice of Coding, check that:

- you have been given the correct allowances;
- the deductions for the State Pension and any untaxed investment income are correct;
- the addition and subtraction are right; and
- the code letter is the appropriate one for your circumstances.

The tax allowances for 2003–2004 were announced in November 2002. So you should have been sent an accurate code for the new tax year before April 2003. If for some reason you did not get a new code for the start of the new tax year on 6 April, your pay or pension office may use the same code as they were using up to 5 April (the last day of the old tax year).

There are other problems that may mean your code is wrong. The Department for Work and Pensions (DWP) should automatically provide information to the Inland Revenue about your State Pension and how much it will be after the April increases. Sometimes, however, the two government departments cannot match up the data and the Inland Revenue is not told exactly how much your pension is. In that case it will work out your new pension from last year's figure. However, that calculation is approximate and may be wrong. So you should always check that the correct amount of pension has been taken into account. If the amount of your State Pension has been overestimated, you should contact your tax office to explain; otherwise you will pay too much tax.

Married Couple's Allowance is a fixed amount deducted from your Income Tax rather than an allowance in the normal sense and cannot be easily taken account of in a tax code. If you get Married Couple's Allowance, you may find your code is reduced by what is called an 'allowance restriction'. This is intended to give you the correct tax relief on your Married Couple's Allowance. However, it may give the wrong answer and you should check at the end of the tax year to see if it has been worked out correctly.

There may be changes in your circumstances which affect your PAYE code. For example:

- starting or giving up work or self-employment;
- getting a new source of income, such as a pension or a lot of investment income;
- your spouse dying;
- getting married – if you or your spouse were born before 6 April 1935;
- separation or divorce;
- reaching 65 or 75 during the tax year; or
- a rise or fall in the untaxed income you get from an investment.

If the number in your code goes up, you will be paying less tax through PAYE; if it goes down, you will be paying more. If you disagree with anything on the Notice of Coding, take a copy of it and send the original back to the tax office, saying what you think is wrong. Alternatively you can phone your tax office to find out more or request that a change should be made.

It is up to you to inform the tax office of any changes which might affect your code and the amount of tax you pay. But even if you do not, remember that the code is only a way of collecting the tax. If you end up paying too much you can claim it back – and if you pay too little, the Inland Revenue can demand it off you later.

When you are sent a Notice of Coding you will also get a leaflet P3(2003) *Understanding your tax code*. You can also get this leaflet from your local tax office, the IR Orderline on 08459 000 404 (calls are charged at local rates) or from the website at www.inlandrevenue.gov.uk/leaflets/c1.htm

SELF-ASSESSMENT

Nearly one and half million pensioners pay their tax through the system called self-assessment. If you are one of them in 2003–2004, you should have been sent a tax return in April 2003. This form relates to your income and allowances for 2002–2003. If you can, it is better to fill in the form and return it by 30 September 2003. The Inland Revenue will then work out the tax you have to pay. If you delay beyond 30 September, then the Revenue will not guarantee to do the calculation in time and you will have to work out the tax due. The absolute deadline for returning the form is 31 January 2004. If you have to pay tax for 2002–2003 it will be due on 31 January 2004. You may also have to make payments on account for 2003–2004 (see below). If you miss these deadlines you may be subject to penalties and interest.

Tax-saving tip: When the self-assessment form arrives, check it contains all the parts you need, return it by the deadline, and pay the tax when it is due.

Who does it affect?

Most older people do not need to worry about self-assessment. But it may affect you if:

- you are self-employed;
- you pay higher-rate tax; or
- your income is above £18,300.

Most older people who pay tax through PAYE and have simple tax affairs will not be sent a tax return and need not worry about self-assessment. However, even if your income is quite low you may still be sent a tax return if you have untaxed income that cannot be collected through PAYE. If you have less than £2,500 of income which is not taxed at source, you may be able to arrange to have this taxed through your PAYE code, rather than filling in a self-assessment return. Your tax office can give you more advice about this.

If you are not usually sent a tax return but have a new source of income or a capital gain on which you need to pay tax, you must tell the Inland Revenue by 5 October after the end of the tax year – thus if you had a new source of income in 2002–2003, you must tell the Inland Revenue by 5 October 2003. You will then be sent a tax return to complete.

When tax is paid

Since the introduction of self-assessment in April 1997 all tax has been based on income received in the current year. The tax is due on 31 January and 31 July, with any balance due the following 31 January. In other words, at the end of January 2004 you are expected to pay half the tax due on income from 6 April 2003 to 5 April 2004. That is clearly impossible to do accurately as you may not know exactly how much your income will be in the time between 1 February and 5 April. So the tax you pay is always an estimate and the payments you make are 'on account' (ie subject to revision). The tax paid is corrected in the following year from the information in your next tax return. The timetable is like this:

April 2003 – tax returns sent out for the tax year 2002–2003. Taxpayer completes with the details of income and allowances for 2002–2003. That information is used to calculate exactly the tax that was due in 2002–2003. You may have already made payments of this tax in January and July 2002.

30 September 2003 – if the form is sent back by this date, the Inland Revenue will calculate the tax due in 2002–2003 and the estimated amount of the tax due in 2003–2004 in time for the 31 January 2004 payment. Even if your return is in later than 30 September, the Revenue will still calculate the tax but may not do so in time. In which case, the taxpayer has to work this out themselves.

31 January 2004 – half the estimated tax for 2003–2004 is due (called a payment on account). In addition any over or under payment for 2002–2003 is corrected. If there was an underpayment, a further payment is due. If there has been an overpayment, then a refund is due. Normally, the extra money or the refund is simply added on or taken off the tax due on account for 2003–2004.

If the balancing payment for 2002–2003 is less than £2,000, it can be collected through PAYE in a future year but only if you get your tax return back by 30 September 2003. If your income goes down significantly from one year to the next, then your estimated tax is likely to be more than the amount actually due. If your circumstances change in this way you can tell the Revenue and pay less on account. However, if it turns out you got it wrong and you pay too little tax, you will be charged interest on the unpaid tax back to the date it was due.

Records

All taxpayers are obliged by law to keep records of their income and capital gains. Unless you are self-employed (see pages 49–56) or rent out property, you can normally destroy records for 2001–2002 – that is those relating to your affairs up to 5 April 2002 – on 6 February 2004. You may have to keep your records longer if the tax return was late or there is an enquiry going on into your tax affairs, or your tax return was sent to you late in the year.

The form

The self-assessment tax returns are sent out after 5 April and ask for information about your income in the previous tax year. Along with the basic tax form, you may receive one or more supplementary pages covering sources of income such as employment, self-employment or rental income. There will also be a guide to completing the form and a separate booklet for the tax calculation. The forms are long and can seem very complicated, so allow yourself plenty of time and ask for help if necessary. You may be able to get help from a local advice agency and you can also ask the Inland Revenue for guidance. However, if your tax affairs are complicated or you cannot manage, you may need to employ an accountant or tax adviser. If you are sent a form you must complete it. If you do not, you could face a penalty. If you want the Inland Revenue to do the calculation, you should send back the form by 30 September; if you miss that deadline there are no penalties but you will have to calculate the tax yourself and get the form in by 31 January. If you miss that deadline you will be fined and if you pay the tax after that date, you may incur interest and surcharges on any tax paid late.

Key dates and penalties – tax returns for 2002–2003

- **April 2003** – tax returns for 2002–2003 sent out to those who need them.
- **30 September 2003** – there is no penalty as such but if your form is not received by this date the Inland Revenue will not guarantee to calculate your tax by the time it is due. Nor can you pay extra tax due through the PAYE system.
- **31 January 2004** – you must send back your tax return by this date. The penalty for missing this date is normally £100 (but if you owe less tax than £100 the penalty cannot be more than the tax due). If you do not owe any tax or you have a reasonable excuse for your return being late, you will not have to pay the penalty.
- **31 January 2004** – balancing payment for 2002–2003 is due and so is the payment on account for the tax year 2003–2004. Penalty interest is charged on unpaid tax on a daily basis. At the start of 2003 this rate was 6.5 per cent a year.
- **28 February 2004** – a 5 per cent surcharge is added onto any tax due for 2002–2003 which is still not paid.
- **28 March 2004** – if the surcharge has not been paid, interest begins to be charged on the surcharge.
- **31 July 2004** – if your tax return has still not been submitted, a second £100 penalty is imposed.
- **31 July 2004** – a further 5 per cent surcharge is added to any tax due for 2002–2003 which is still not paid.

- **28 August 2004** – if the further surcharge has not been paid, interest begins to be charged on it.

For further information see Inland Revenue leaflet SA/BK8 *Self-assessment: your guide*. Leaflets SA/BK6 and SA/BK7 cover penalties and surcharges, and SA/BK3 and SA/BK4 cover record keeping. You can also contact the Inland Revenue's Self-Assessment Helpline on 0845 9000 444.

After you send in your tax return

If you have asked the Inland Revenue to calculate your tax bill, or you have calculated your tax but the Inland Revenue has changed your figures, you will be sent a Tax Calculation. You should check that the figures are correct and that you agree with any changes made. If you want to amend anything you should let the Inland Revenue know as quickly as possible. Everyone who is sent a tax return has a 'tax account' opened at the Inland Revenue. You will receive a Statement of Account showing the money you owe and also in certain other circumstances, including:

- when there are changes to items in your account;
- when a tax payment is due in the next 35 days;
- every two months when between £32 and £500 is due;
- every month when over £500 is due;
- when the Inland Revenue has arranged for unpaid tax to be collected through PAYE; or
- when you have paid more tax than is due.

You should check your Statement of Account when you receive it and contact the Inland Revenue if you disagree with the entries. A small number of tax returns are selected for investigation – they are called 'enquiries'. Usually this is because something appears wrong, or if the figures have changed significantly from one year to the next, but some tax returns are selected at random.

Tax-saving tip: Even if you get your form in by 30 September and the Inland Revenue works out your tax, check it. The Revenue admits that it gets around half a million self-assessment calculations wrong.

CLAIMING TAX BACK

If you think you may have paid too much tax, you can claim it back. If you have not been given the correct allowance or if tax has wrongly been deducted from interest or other income, you should claim it back at once. You can claim for the current year 2003–2004 and up to six years back – right back to 1997–1998. If you think that the Inland Revenue has made a mistake, you can go back even further.

There are many circumstances in which the amount of tax you pay may be wrong.

When you leave work

When you retire from work, your income will usually fall. If that happens during the tax year you may qualify for a tax rebate. If the State Pension is your only income when you retire, send your P45 form to your tax office, including details of your age, the date you retired, and your estimated total income from the day you retire until the next 5 April. If any refund is due, it will normally come directly from the tax office. If you get a pension from an ex-employer, any tax rebate due for the tax year in which you retired will normally be paid by reducing the tax due on your occupational pension. If information is not received by the end of the tax year when you retired, any rebate will normally come direct from the tax office.

Tax-saving tip: If your income falls significantly during the tax year, make sure that the tax office knows.

Savings and investment income

Unless you have applied to get your interest paid gross, any savings or investment income such as interest on a bank or building society account will automatically have had 20 per cent tax deducted from it. If you have not used up all of your tax allowances, or you are only due to pay 10 per cent tax on some or all of this income, you can apply for a repayment.

Non-taxpayers with dividend income can no longer claim back tax credits for dividends paid after April 1999 but can still claim overpaid tax for the two tax years 1997–1998 and 1998–1999.

If the total amount of tax overpaid is £50 or less, you should apply at the end of the tax year; if the tax owed is more than £50, you can apply for a repayment during the year on claim form R40. If you make a claim each year, you should receive claim form R40 automatically. If you have not previously claimed, get form R40 from your tax office or an Inland Revenue Enquiry Centre.

Inland Revenue booklet IR 110 *Bank and building society interest: A guide for savers* gives more information about claiming back tax. You can ring the Taxback Helpline on 0845 077 6543 (calls are charged at local rates).

Personal circumstances

If your personal circumstances change, you may end up paying too much tax. Marriage, divorce, widowhood, taking on responsibilities for a child, becoming blind, or reaching 65 or 75 can all affect the tax you pay.

Tax-saving tip: If your personal circumstances change, check with the tax office to see if it affects your tax position.

Payments to charity

If you pay higher-rate tax you should keep a receipt for any money you pay to a charity, and that can include any single gift or a subscription. The basic-rate tax is reclaimed by the charity, but you can reclaim the higher-rate tax – which equals 23 per cent of the amount you gave, through your self-assessment tax return.

UNDERPAYMENT OF TAX

If you have not paid enough tax in the current or previous tax years – perhaps because of an oversight on your part – then you may owe tax. Many older people whose tax affairs are straightforward do not receive a tax return every year. So if you have recently started to receive income from a new source, such as savings or investments, the Inland Revenue may not be aware of it. If you think that you may have income which you have not reported, contact your tax office and explain. Normally, you have to tell the Inland Revenue about any new source of income by 5 October in the tax year after it is received. So if you have new income in the tax year 2003–2004, you must tell the Revenue by 5 October 2004. The Inland Revenue can go back for up to six tax years, or longer in the case of negligence or fraud, to examine your income and the tax due. You may have to pay a surcharge and interest on late payments.

People who have deliberately evaded tax or who have seriously neglected their tax affairs may be liable to penalties. In the very rare cases where this amounts to fraud, the Inland Revenue may bring criminal proceedings.

Inland Revenue delay

If the Inland Revenue has been very slow in dealing with your tax affairs or in taking into account information it has been given, and later discovers that you have not paid enough tax, you may not have to pay the difference. You could qualify for what is known as 'Extra-Statutory Concession A19'. This concession applies where the Inland Revenue fails to act on information supplied by you, your employer or the Department for Work and Pensions, and you could reasonably have believed that your tax affairs were in order. However, the concession is not normally given if you were notified of the arrears in the tax year in which they arose or by the end of the following tax year.

DEALING WITH THE INLAND REVENUE

The Inland Revenue is the government department which deals with almost all the taxes due in the UK. Which tax office handles your affairs will depend on your circumstances. If you are still in paid work, it will be your employer's tax office; if you are self-employed, it will usually be the office covering the location of your business; if you are unemployed or retired, it may be your last employer's tax office; if you are receiving a pension or annuity, it will usually be the office dealing with the pension provider. Sometimes more than one tax office may be involved but there will always be one main office which should coordinate your tax affairs.

It is likely that your tax office will not be nearby, so you will have to contact it by letter or telephone. When writing you should always include your tax reference number, or your National Insurance number, which you will find on papers you have received from the Inland Revenue. Keep correspondence you receive and you should always take a copy of letters and papers you send. Contacting your tax office by telephone may be quicker and easier, however, and if you are worried about the cost you can ask to be rung back. After a telephone conversation it is sensible to follow it up with a letter to confirm what was said, and ask the tax office to do the same.

Getting help and advice

If you need help with your tax affairs, you can also ask at a local tax office or Inland Revenue Enquiry Centre (look in the phone book under 'Inland Revenue'). This may be easier than contacting your own tax office as it will probably be closer, so you could talk to someone face to face. If you cannot get out, the office may be able to arrange a home visit. If you have hearing difficulties, the Revenue can provide services such as textphone and typetalk, although not all offices have these. You could also seek help from a local agency such as a Citizens Advice Bureau. However, if your tax position is complicated, perhaps because you are self-employed or have considerable investment income, you will probably need to employ an accountant or tax adviser. TaxAid is a charity that provides a free and independent advisory service to people with tax problems who cannot afford an accountant or tax adviser – see page 171 for details of how to contact TaxAid.

The Inland Revenue produces a number of leaflets about tax which can be obtained from any Inland Revenue Enquiry Centre. To find your nearest office, look under 'Inland Revenue' in your local phone book. Leaflets can be provided in Braille, audio and large print on request. Almost all of them are available on the Inland Revenue website at www.inlandrevenue.gov.uk or from the Orderline on 08459 000 404 (calls are charged at local rates).

Appeals and complaints

If you disagree with a decision about your tax, you can appeal against it. For example, you may think you have been incorrectly charged a late filing penalty on your tax return. You appeal by writing to the Inspector of Taxes at your tax office. You should do this within 30 days of receiving the decision you disagree with. Often appeals are settled by agreement but you have the right to take a case to an independent tribunal. This is intended to be an informal process and you cannot be asked to pay costs. Further information is given in Inland Revenue leaflet IR 37 *Appeals against tax.*

The Inland Revenue's Service Commitment sets out the kind of service you can expect from the Inland Revenue. Leaflet IR 167 *Charter for Inland Revenue taxpayers* gives details about what the Commitment says and what you should do if you are not satisfied with the way your tax affairs have been handled. There is also COP1 *Putting things right when we make mistakes,* which contains a lot of useful information.

If the Revenue does make a mistake that causes you expense, you can reclaim this money. You may also get a payment of between £25 to £500 to compensate you for distress and inconvenience.

If you are not satisfied with the Inland Revenue's response to a complaint, there is an Adjudicator's Office which can consider the matter and recommend appropriate action. The Adjudicator is independent of the Inland Revenue. Alternatively, you can refer a complaint to the Parliamentary Ombudsman through your MP.

For further information see leaflet AO1 *How to complain about the Inland Revenue and the Valuation Office Agency*. Copies are available from tax offices or phone the Adjudicator's Office on 020 7930 2292 or look at the website at www.adjudicatorsoffice.gov.uk

---

TAX FOR SELF-EMPLOYED PEOPLE

If you work for yourself you should be treated as self-employed for tax purposes. In that case, you will be dealt with under self-assessment and have to work out your own profits and pay your own Income Tax. If you are under pension age, you may also have to pay your own National Insurance contributions (NICs); if your annual turnover is more than £56,000 you may also have to charge Value Added Tax (VAT) on your invoices and pay that to Customs & Excise. If your turnover is less than £150,000 you may benefit from the flat-rate scheme (see page 43) – ask your VAT office.

Income Tax

Income from self-employment is added to income from pensions and other sources to determine the total amount of tax you are liable to pay. You will have self-employed income if you are in business on your own account, even on a part-time or occasional basis, and the money you earn exceeds your business expenses.

Notifying the Inland Revenue

If you become self-employed, you are now legally obliged to notify the Inland Revenue when you start. Registration is required for both Income Tax and National Insurance and you can register for both at the same time. If you do not register within the first three full months of self-employment, you may be liable for a penalty of £100. If you have still not registered by 6 October following the end of the tax year when you start up, further penalties may be due. Further details are given in the Inland Revenue leaflet P/SE/1, *Thinking of working for yourself?*

You can notify the Inland Revenue that you are self-employed simply by writing to your local tax office; always keep a copy of any letter you send. A better method may be to obtain leaflet P/SE/1 and fill in form CWF1 which it contains. You can also register by phone – call the Revenue Helpline for the Newly Self-employed on 08459 15 45 15.

Your accounting date

Once the Inland Revenue knows you are self-employed, you should be sent a self-assessment form each April, including the pages for self-employment. On this you must declare your business income and expenses. The balance of your income, less your expenses, is your taxable profit – in other words it is the income on which you are liable to pay tax.

Although the Income Tax year runs from 6 April to the following 5 April, you can fix your own 'accounting year' over which you work out your income and expenses and arrive at your profit or loss. For any tax year, your tax calculation will be based on your profit for the 12 months up to your accounting date which ends in that tax year. When you start in self-employment it can be worthwhile to fix your accounting year to end on 30 April. This year, for example, that would mean the profit from the year 1 May 2002 to 30 April 2003 is taxed in the tax year 2003–2004. If your accounting year runs from 1 April 2002 to 31 March 2003 (ie just a month earlier), that income would be taxed a whole year earlier in 2002–2003. So by fixing your accounting year to end on 30 April, you in effect put off the tax you pay by almost a year. It also means that you know the exact figures when you come to fill in your tax return.

When a business starts and ends

Special rules apply in the first two years of a new business and when a business ends. For the first year you are taxed on your profit from the date you start until the following 5 April. For the second year you are taxed on your profit for the 12 months up to your accounting date in that tax year, provided that the date is at least a year after your business started. If it is not, you are taxed on your profit for the first 12 months of business.

These rules may mean that some part of your profit is taken into account in calculating your taxable profit for more than one tax year. If so, you are entitled to 'overlap relief' when your business ends, the effect being that, over the lifetime of your business, you are taxed on no more and no less than the full amount of your profit. All this gets very complex and it is worth consulting an accountant, at least in the first and last years of your business.

Tax-saving tip: Choose your accounting date to reduce the tax you pay. When your business starts and ends, get the tax you pay carefully checked by an accountant.

Business expenses

There is normally no difficulty in deciding how much your business income is, but working out your expenses may be more difficult. The situation is fairly clear-cut if, for example, you are buying goods to resell, but determining other expenses is less straightforward – particularly when expenses are partly for business purposes and partly private.

For example, if you work from home you need a telephone. Unless you go to the expense of having a separate business line, your calls will be a mixture of business and personal. The cost of business calls will be a tax-deductible expense and so will a share of the phone rental. To work out the share get an itemised bill, which BT and most other phone companies provide at no cost. You can then see the proportion of the costs that are business. There is no need to count them up each time; do it once and then in future you can just charge that proportion of your bill to the business. Keep the evidence in case the Revenue queries it. It is sensible to monitor the position from time to time, especially if the business grows. You can also charge a proportion of the cost of running your car. Keep a note of business and personal mileage to work out the business share.

If you work from home, you will also be able to claim a proportion of domestic expenses such as gas, electricity, water, and even rent as a business expense. The normal way to work out the proportion is to count the main rooms in the house, excluding the kitchen and bathroom. If there are four main rooms and you mainly work from one of them, and use that room for little else, then charge a quarter of the costs to the business – but see pages 55–56.

Tax-saving tip: Whenever you buy anything which is for your business (even a newspaper or magazine) or you spend anything on travel (even a bus fare), get a receipt and keep it.

Capital allowances

The costs of major items, such as a vehicle or office equipment, are normally not all tax-deductible in the year in which you made the expenditure. Instead, tax relief is given through a system of 'capital allowances', which means that the cost of the equipment is spread over a number of years. You can charge 40 per cent of the cost as an expense in the first year and 25 per cent of the balance in the years after that. The 40 per cent rate does not apply to vehicles such as cars. Until 31 March 2004 the capital cost of computers and related equipment as well as software and advanced technology mobile telephones can all be counted as an expense in just one year. That is known as a 100 per cent capital allowance. The rules and arithmetic of capital allowances are complex, so advice from an accountant or even the Inland Revenue can save you money.

Tax-saving tip: If you buy anything for your business which will last, you must count it as a capital expense. You can get 40 per cent of the cost in year one. But the allowance in the first year for cars is 25 per cent.

Inland Revenue Self-assessment Help Sheet IR 222 gives information about business expenses and capital allowances. It can be ordered on the IR Orderline on 08459 000 404.

Keeping records

On your tax return, you are simply expected to declare total income and expenses. The Inland Revenue does not normally expect to see invoices, receipts, etc. Nor does it expect to be sent accounts prepared by an accountant. However, you must keep proper records of all these things so that you can work out your income and expenditure. You must also keep all your bank or building society statements or passbooks. It is essential that you have an accounts book, and write it up regularly. If you keep records on your computer, you should always back up the files and print them out regularly. If you have an internet bank or savings account, print out your statements each month and keep them in a file.

If you are self-employed or rent out property, you are legally obliged to keep all records relating to a particular tax year for five years from the date you filed your return for that year. You can now burn records for the year 1996–1997. The tax return for the following year, 1997–1998, was due in to the Inland Revenue by 31 January 1999. Five years from then is 31 January 2004. So you can burn your self-employment records from 1997–1998 on 1 February 2004. However, if the Inland Revenue has embarked on an enquiry into your tax affairs you have to keep the relevant records until that enquiry is finished.

For more details see Inland Revenue leaflet SA/BK3 *Self-assessment: a guide to keeping records for the self-employed.*

When tax is paid

Tax on income from self-employment is normally paid in two instalments and a balancing payment. For the 2003–2004 tax year, the first instalment will be due on 31 January 2004 and the second on 31 July 2004. If it turns out you have paid too little tax, then a balancing payment will become due on 31 January 2005. The amount of tax payable under the first two instalments is based upon the amount of tax you were liable to pay for the previous year. Half that amount will normally be due in each instalment. If, however, you believe that your tax will be less than that for the previous year, you can apply to your tax office to have the instalments reduced. If the total tax due is less than £500, no instalment payments will be required and you can pay all of it on 31 January 2005. If you do not pay the correct amount of tax on the proper date, you will be liable to pay interest on unpaid tax.

National Insurance contributions

If you work and earn £89 a week or more you will have to pay National Insurance contributions. They will normally be deducted from your pay before you get it. However, these contributions stop when you reach State Pension age – currently 60 for a woman, 65 for a man.

Tax-saving tip: Once you reach 60 or 65 check that no National Insurance contributions are being deducted from your pay. They should stop in the week of your birthday.

If you are self-employed and are below pension age, then you may have to pay two separate National Insurance contributions – they are called Class 2 and Class 4.

Class 2 contributions are £2 a week in the 2003–2004 tax year. If you reach pension age during a tax year, you can stop paying Class 2 in the week you reach that age. Class 2 contributions are either paid quarterly, or when you are sent a bill, or by monthly direct debit. Leaflet P/SE/1 includes a direct debit mandate you can use. You will be exempt from Class 2 contributions if you expect your annual profit to be below a certain limit, which for the 2003–2004 tax year is £4,095. An application for this 'Small Earnings Exception' should be sent to the Inland Revenue National Insurance Contributions Office (NICO) in advance. In practice the Office may agree to backdate an application.

Class 4 contributions are collected by the Inland Revenue with your Income Tax. Contributions are charged at 8 per cent on profits between £4,615 and £30,940 in 2003–2004 and at 1 per cent on income above that. You have to pay Class 4 contributions for the whole tax year in which you reach pension age but not after that.

If you have income from paid employment as well as from self-employment, and you are under pension age, you will be paying Class 1 contributions which are deducted straight from your earnings. There are complex rules which determine the total amount of National Insurance contributions you have to pay and your Class 2 and Class 4 contributions may be reduced. If this is likely to apply to you, you should seek advice from NICO.

Tax-saving tip: If you are employed and self-employed, check that you are not paying too much in National Insurance contributions.

For more information see Inland Revenue leaflet CWL2 *National Insurance contributions for self-employed people.*

Value Added Tax

If you are self-employed, or run a small business, you will have to register for VAT if your annual gross business income (your turnover) exceeds a certain limit (£56,000 for the 2003–2004 tax year). Once registered, you will have to charge VAT on any goods or services you supply at the standard rate of 17.5 per cent. You can also reclaim the VAT you pay on goods or services you buy. Each quarter (or annually if your turnover is low and you prefer to do it that way) you submit a VAT return showing the amount of VAT collected from your customers and the amount you are reclaiming on goods or services you have bought. You then send a cheque for the net VAT – or make a claim for a refund if you have paid more VAT than you have collected.

If your turnover is £150,000 or less you may want to pay your VAT under the flat-rate scheme. Instead of working out the VAT you have charged and spent and paying the difference to Customs & Excise, you can pay a flat-rate percentage of your turnover. The percentages range from about 6 per cent to about 17 per cent, depending on your category of business. There is more information on the Customs and Excise website at www.hmce.gov.uk

Money-saving tip: In some circumstances, even if your gross business income does not exceed the £56,000 limit, it may be desirable to register for VAT. If you do register you will be able to recover the VAT on goods or services you buy for business purposes and that will cut your costs.

HOW TO CHECK YOUR TAX BILL

This section of the book shows you how to check that you are paying the right amount of Income Tax.

If you follow the steps below, you should be able to see if you should pay tax and how much you are due to pay. Before you do that, however, there is one thing to understand. Your income comes in two sorts and each sort is taxed differently. First there is income from investments – that is like the cream and always sits on the top of your income. At the very top of the cream is the double cream of your dividends. Second, sitting under the cream, is the milk of all your other income. Tax allowances and rates of tax are applied from the bottom up. So the allowances or the tax applies first to your other income and then to income from investments.

Step 1   List all your income separately in two columns – investment income in column a, and all the rest (such as pensions and earnings) in column b. Delete all the income that is tax-free (see pages 4–6). Make sure that all the remaining income is listed gross (ie before tax is deducted). For income that you receive tax-paid, such as interest on money in a bank or building society, gross it up by dividing by 4 and multiplying by 5. If you have dividend income, divide it by 9 and multiply by 10. Add up each column (a and b) separately to get total a and total b, and then add them together to get your 'total income'.

Step 2   Look up your Personal Allowance on page 15. If you are aged 65 or over and your total income is less than £18,300 you can claim the full Personal Allowance for your age. If it is more than £18,300, reduce the allowance by £1 for every £2 above but do not reduce your Personal Allowance below £4,615. If you are blind, add on the £1,510 Blind Person's Allowance too. Do not add on the Married Couple's Allowance even if you are entitled to it. It is dealt with at step 6. Allowances are explained on pages 15–19.

Step 3   If your tax allowance is more than your total income, then no tax is due.

- If you subtract your allowance from your total income and you get less than £1,960, then your tax is just 10 per cent of the answer. Skip steps 4 and 5 and go straight to step 6.

- Otherwise, separate out your income into the two columns a (interest) and b (other income). If the allowance is less than the amount in column b, subtract it and write down the result. Then go straight to step 4. If the allowance is more than the amount in column b, then subtract the total in column b from the allowance and subtract that answer from the total in column a. Skip step 4 and go straight to step 5.

Step 4   The first £1,960 of your income above the allowances is taxed at 10 per cent. If there is other income left above that, the next slice up to £28,540 (a total of £30,500) is taxed at 22 per cent. If there is more above that, it is taxed at 40 per cent. When you run out of other income, look at your income in column a (interest). If you have taxed any income at 40 per cent, deduct any income from dividends and tax the savings income at 40 per cent and the dividend income at 22.5 per cent. Otherwise, ignore the dividend income and tax the rest at 20 per cent. Now skip step 5 and go to step 6.

Step 5   You reached this step because your tax-free allowance used up all your 'other' column b income. You should have deducted the balance of your allowance from your investment income in column a. Deduct any income from dividends. Now, the first £1,960 of your remaining investment is taxed at 10 per cent. If there is other income left above that, the next slice up to £28,540 above the £1,960 is taxed at 20 per cent. If there is more above that, it is taxed at 40 per cent. If you tax any income at 40 per cent, then tax your gross dividends at 22.5 per cent – otherwise do not tax them at all.

Step 6   If you qualify for a Married Couple's Allowance, calculate 10 per cent of this allowance. Deduct this amount from the tax you are due to pay. The balance is the tax you should pay altogether in 2003–2004. Much or all of this tax will already have been paid either through PAYE or through the automatic deduction of tax from investment income.

Step 7 Add up the tax that has already been deducted from the interest paid on a bank or building society account. Deduct that total from the tax you are due to pay. If it is bigger than the tax you are due to pay, then you may be due some tax back. **Apply for a refund**. If it is smaller, this is the amount of tax you still have to pay. Check how much tax has been deducted through PAYE. If it is more than the tax due, **apply for a refund**.

Examples

1. Single person

Joan Miller, 77, gets the Basic State Pension, which includes some graduated retirement benefit, and totals £81.35 a week. She also has a small pension from her former employer of £135 a month, gross. In addition she expects to receive £20 interest from a National Savings and Investments ordinary account. She checks her building society account and finds that she has earned £375 gross and that £75 has already been deducted in tax. Joan follows the steps set out above to work out her tax for the 2003–2004 tax year.

Step 1 She writes down all her income, remembering to use the gross amount of her building society interest. Her £20 interest on her National Savings ordinary account is not taxable. She crosses that out and adds up her other income:

State Pension	£4,230.20
Pension from employer	£1,620.00
Interest on savings, gross	£375.00
Total income	£6,225.20

Step 2 As Joan is over 75 she is entitled to the highest level of Personal Allowance. As her total income is less than £18,300, she can claim the full higher allowance for someone over 75 of £6,720.

Step 3 Joan's income of £6,225.20 is less than her Personal Allowance of £6,720. So no tax is due. However, Joan has had £75 deducted from her building society interest. She checks back and finds this has happened every year. So she claims back the overpaid tax, on Form R40, back to 1997–1998 (it comes to more than £300). She also fills in form R85 so that in future her interest is paid gross.

Tax-saving tip: If you are not liable to pay tax, then you should not have tax deducted from interest on your savings in a bank or building society account.

2. Married couple

Ravi Patel is 69 and married to Sangeeta, who is 63. They must look at their tax positions separately.

Step 1 Ravi has retired and receives a State Pension of £98.05 a week which includes some SERPS (officially called Additional Pension) from a previous job. He also receives a reasonable occupational pension from his last employer of £530 a month gross. He and Sangeeta have a joint building society account on which they received net interest of £484. The Inland Revenue will treat this as being split equally between them; ie £242 each, which is grossed up as £242/4 × 5 = £302.50. Ravi works out his total income for 2003–2004:

State Pension	£5,098.60
Pension from employer	£6,360.00
Half interest on savings, grossed up	£302.50
Total income	**£11,761.10**

Step 2 Ravi is entitled to a Personal Allowance for someone aged 65–74. As his total income is below £18,300, he gets the full allowance for people aged 65–74, which is £6,610.

Step 3 Ravi's income is more than his Personal Allowance, so some tax is due. He separates his income into savings and other income and deducts the Personal Allowance of £6,610 from his other income of £11,458.60 – without his interest – which leaves £4,848.60.

Step 4 10 per cent of the first £1,960 = £196.00

22 per cent of the remaining £2,888.60 = £635.49

He then adds on 20 per cent of his £302.50 gross savings income = £60.50

Total tax due in this step is £891.99.

Step 5 He skips.

Step 6 Ravi is 69 in July 2003, so he was born before 6 April 1935, and can get the Married Couple's Allowance, which at his age is £5,565. So his tax bill is reduced by 10 per cent of that (£556.50). He deducts this from the tax due in step 4 of £891.99–£556.50 = £335.49. So that figure is the tax he should have paid. He has already paid his share of the tax on his building society account which amounts to £60.50, so he should only have tax of £335.49–£60.50 = £274.99 deducted from his pension at the rate of £22.91 a month. When he checks he finds that he has had more than this deducted, so he claims a refund.

Sangeeta then does her tax.

Step 1 Sangeeta has recently retired from full-time work but does not get a pension from her former employer. She gets a State Pension of £46.35 a week paid on Ravi's contributions. She is still working part-time, 15 hours a week at £4.70 an hour. And she has her share of the interest on their joint savings – £302.50 gross.

She adds up her income:

State Pension	£2,410.20
Earnings	£3,666.00
Half interest on savings, grossed up	£302.50
Total income	£6,378.70

Step 2 Sangeeta is under 65 so she is entitled to the basic Personal Allowance of £4,615.

Step 3 Sangeeta's total taxable income is more than her Personal Allowance, so tax is due. The difference is only £1,763.70, which is less than £1,960. So she taxes the £1,763.70 at 10 per cent.

Sangeeta's tax so far is:

10 per cent of £1,763.70 = £176.37

She skips to **Step 6** She is not entitled to a Married Couple's Allowance – Ravi has that and she does not need any transferred to her. She checks her wages and finds that over the year she has paid £146.12 in tax. She has also had tax at 20 per cent deducted automatically from her interest. Her share of that is £60.50. Altogether she has paid £206.62 tax (around £30 too much). So she claims £30 back from the Inland Revenue. She finds her local Tax Enquiry Office in the phone book and gets form R40, fills it in and sends it off. She is delighted to find that she also gets some money back for previous years too.

Tax-saving tip: If you are only due to pay tax at 10 per cent, then you can claim back half the tax you have had deducted from your bank or building society interest.

3 Married couple with one spouse paying no tax

Sid Jones is 69 and his wife Lillian is 67. In 2003–2004 Sid receives the State Pension, which in his case is £84 a week, and a pension from his job of £1,160 a month. Sid also put a lump sum in the building society when he retired and that brought in £1,200 in 2003–2004, which they found very useful. Sid grosses it up, which means he counts £1,500 as his income. Lillian only gets the married woman's pension which is £46.35 a week, or £2,410.20 a year, which is less than her Personal Allowance of £6,610, so she pays no tax. Sid, however, pays quite a lot.

Step 1 He adds up his total income:

State Pension	£4,368
Occupational pension	£13,920
Building society interest (gross)	£1,500
Total income	**£19,788**

Step 2 Sid is 69 and so he should be entitled to the higher Personal Allowance of £6,610. However, Sid's gross income of £19,788 is more than the income limit of £18,300 for the higher levels of Personal Allowance. He takes one from the other and gets £1,488, so he halves that, and deducts the £744 from his Personal Allowance of £6,610 to get £5,866, which is his Personal Allowance for 2003–2004.

Step 3 Sid has to pay tax and he has to pay it on more than £1,960 so he subtracts his Personal Allowance of £5,866 from his 'other' income (£4,368 + £13,920), which leaves £12,422.

Step 4 The first £1,960 is taxed at 10 per cent and the rest is taxed at 22 per cent. His savings income is taxed at 20 per cent.

10 per cent of the first £1,960 taxable income	£196.00
22 per cent of the remaining £10,462	£2,301.64
20 per cent of interest of £1,500	£300.00
Total tax bill	**£2,797.64**

Step 6 Sid's Married Couple's Allowance is £5,565, and provides 10 per cent tax relief. His tax bill is therefore reduced by 10 per cent of £5,565, which is £556.50. Total tax due is £2,767.64 – £556.50 = £2,241.14.

Sid checks his tax and finds he has paid tax on his savings through the automatic deduction by the building society. His tax on his State Pension and his occupational pension was deducted through PAYE from his occupational pension. He finds it is not quite right – he actually has not paid quite enough tax because the coding could not cope with the reduction in his Personal Allowance.

Sid tells the tax office but is advised that he could actually pay less tax is if he transferred the money in his building society account to Lillian. If he had done so before the start of the tax year, Lillian's income would then have consisted of the State Pension of £2,410.20 plus the interest of £1,500. This total of £3,910.20 is still well below her Personal Allowance of £6,610 and so no tax is due on it. As a non-taxpayer she could have applied to have the interest paid without the tax being deducted. That will save them the £300 tax due on the interest. But the savings don't stop there. Sid's total income would then have been £18,288 which is below the £18,300 limit for the age allowance. So he would get the full higher Personal Allowance of £6,610. That cuts his tax bill by a further £163.68, so altogether he saves £463.68 (nearly £9 a week). Sid and Lillian have a holiday on the proceeds.

Tax-saving tip: If one partner pays no tax or tax at a lower rate, you can save tax by transferring income or savings to that partner.

Before you do this, remember that although transferring assets can save tax, there can also be disadvantages. For example, if Sid gave all his savings to Lillian and then she had to go into a care home, those savings would mean she got no help with her fees. If you do transfer assets, this must be a genuine gift, so the recipient has complete control over the asset – you must not keep an interest in it yourself.

CAPITAL GAINS TAX

You may have to pay some Capital Gains Tax (CGT) if you sell or give away an asset which has increased in value since you bought it. An 'asset' is something you own, such as shares, antiques or property. It is not money as such. The profit on which you are taxed is called a capital gain. However, not all gains are taxed. Some items are free of CGT:

- your only or main private residence (see page 55);
- private cars;
- National Savings certificates;
- most British Government stocks;
- personal belongings worth up to £6,000;
- Individual Savings Accounts (ISAs) and Personal Equity Plans (PEPs);
- proceeds of most life insurance policies;
- premium bond prizes, betting winnings, National Lottery winnings; and
- gifts to registered charities.

How CGT is calculated

Two further exemptions limit the amount which any individual pays in CGT:

- Any gift you make to a husband or wife whom you live with is entirely free of CGT. However, if they then dispose of the asset, tax is due and will be calculated from the date on which you acquired it.
- In the tax year 2003–2004 you can have up to £7,900 of capital gains without paying tax. Husbands and wives are taxed independently on any gains, and each partner is entitled to a separate exempt amount of £7,900.

Anything above the limit is added to your income and taxed as though it was sitting on top of your income. So depending how much other income you have, your gains will be taxed either at 10 per cent, 20 per cent or 40 per cent. Although it is taxed as income, if you have a low income you cannot use your personal Income Tax allowance to reduce a capital gain.

If you disposed of an asset before 6 April 1998 the amount of chargeable gain would have been calculated using a system known as 'indexation'. Under indexation the selling price or market value is reduced by the amount of inflation over the period you owned the asset.

A new system was introduced from April 1998 onwards. Indexation is replaced by a taper which will reduce the amount of gain that is chargeable according to how long you have held the asset. For example for non-business assets owned for five years since April 1998, 85 per cent of the gain will be chargeable, and if they are held for 10 or more years the figure will be 60 per cent. If you acquired the asset before April 1998, indexation will apply to the period from when you acquired it up until April 1998 and the taper will apply to gains after that date. There is a more rapid taper for business assets.

Certain expenses can also be deducted, including the cost of acquiring or disposing of the asset, or of repairing it. Your total capital gains in a year can be reduced if you have also made capital losses – for example if you bought shares which are now worth less and you sell them. Losses from earlier years can be carried forward. If your overall net gain is £7,900 or less there will be no CGT to pay.

Assets acquired before 31 March 1982 involve slightly different calculations, so you should get advice from an accountant.

Windfalls

Recently some mutual insurance companies have been sold and members of the company have received large windfalls from the proceeds. If windfalls – added to any other capital gains – exceed £7,900 in the tax year, then CGT will be due. The Inland Revenue argument is that it cost you nothing to become a member of the mutual company, but that membership is now worth a lot of money. So the value of the membership has grown and that is a capital gain. Two insurance companies have devised a way to avoid CGT by lending you the money and paying you interest on it, allowing you to cash in the loan each year in chunks that are below the CGT limit. Others may follow suit.

Tax-saving tip: If you are married, you can double the amount you cash in each year. Gifts of a loan to a spouse incur no CGT and they can then cash them in.

Your home

Capital Gains Tax is not normally charged when you sell or give away the home you live in, as long as:

- it has been your 'main' residence throughout your ownership; and
- the grounds do not exceed half a hectare (which is a bit more than one acre).

If you own and live in two properties, you can nominate one of them to be your 'main' residence. You need to do this within two years of acquiring the second property. If the other property has been occupied by a dependent relative rent-free since before 6 April 1988, it may be exempt from CGT.

If you have a lodger in the home you own, who shares a kitchen and bathroom and living space with you and who lives as a member of the family, you should not have to pay CGT when you sell the property. However, if you let part of your home to someone who does not live as a member of your family, CGT may be payable. That applies even if the rent is exempt from Income Tax under the Rent a Room scheme (see page 152). The gain on which CGT will be calculated is related to the proportion of the property that is rented and the period of letting relative to the total period of ownership. However, a certain amount of the gain will normally be exempt so you may not have to pay any CGT. Ask at your tax office if you need further details.

If you use part of your home exclusively for business purposes, then a proportion of the property may also be liable to CGT when you sell it.

Tax-saving tip: If you use a room to run a small business or for self-employment, make sure you use it for something else as well.

Selling your business

From April 2003 there is no special relief when you sell a business on retirement or due to ill-health.

Selling your shares

Shares, unit trust units and shares in OEICs (see pages 105–106) give rise to capital gains or losses when you sell them or give them away. But when you sell or give away shares of the same type in the same company which you acquired at different times, there are special rules which govern the way gains and losses are worked out. This does not apply to shares or unit trusts held as part of an ISA or a PEP, which are exempt from tax.

If you give shares to someone else who is not your spouse then the difference between the price you paid and their current market value is treated as a capital gain. If it exceeds your allowances, then you will be liable for CGT.

For more information, see Inland Revenue leaflet CGT1 *Capital Gains Tax: an introduction* or contact your tax office.

INHERITANCE TAX

Inheritance Tax (IHT) may have to be paid on your estate when you die. In some circumstances, gifts you made in the seven years before you die may also count as part of your estate and be taxed. However, the vast majority of estates are not liable to estate duty. As long as the total you left and gave away within seven years is less than £255,000, no tax is due. If the death occurred before 6 April 2003, lower limits apply. No Inheritance Tax is due on anything left to your wife or husband.

Gifts made more than seven years before your death are completely exempt from IHT. Other gifts are also not counted, including:

- gifts to your husband or wife;
- wedding gifts of up to £5,000 to your child, or £2,500 to your grandchild or great-grandchild, or £1,000 to anyone else;
- small gifts of up to £250 each to any number of people;
- regular gifts out of income that do not reduce your standard of living;
- gifts to a major political party, a registered charity, a national museum or art gallery, or a university; and
- other gifts totalling no more than £3,000 in a year. You can also carry this allowance forward from the previous year.

These allowances are personal – so a husband and wife can each give these amounts.

Tax-saving tip: If you have made no gifts to reduce IHT, a husband and wife can give away £12,000 in one tax year without it counting for IHT at all. Even if all the assets are owned by one partner, they can give £6,000 to their spouse, which will be exempt, and then each can give £6,000 to a child for example.

How IHT is calculated

To find out whether your heirs are likely to face a bill on your estate, do the following calculations:

- Add up the value of everything you own, including your house, any investments, savings, personal property, and the value of any life insurance policies.
- Add to that any gifts you have made in the past seven years, but do not include any gifts which are covered by the exemptions listed above.
- Take away any money owed on your mortgage or any other debts. (When you die, unpaid bills, taxes, reasonable funeral expenses, etc, will be deducted from your estate.)
- Take away from the total anything you intend to leave to your spouse or to charity.

If the final amount is less than the threshold for IHT, currently £255,000, no tax will be due. If your total is more than this, it is likely that there will be IHT to pay. It is due at one rate of 40 per cent on the excess over the threshold.

Reducing IHT

It is possible to plan ahead to reduce the IHT which is due:

- If you have a life insurance policy that pays out on your death, make sure that the policy is what is called 'written in trust'. That means that the proceeds do not go directly to your dependants. Instead they are paid into a trust which then passes them onto your dependants – that avoids the proceeds counting as part of your estate.
- If you own your home jointly with your spouse or partner, make sure that it is owned as 'beneficial tenants in common' rather than as 'joint tenants'. If you own it as tenants in common, each of you owns half of it and can leave that half separately to your heirs. If you own it as joint tenants, then when one dies the other automatically owns the whole property. When they subsequently die, the whole property forms part of their estate and tax may be due.
- If there is a danger of IHT being due, then use your exemptions every year to give away money or property. But beware about giving away shares or anything which may

have grown in value. If you do that, then Capital Gains Tax may be payable. It is safer to give away money.

- Trusts can be a way to avoid IHT but they are expensive to set up and run and are really only suitable for people with estates worth considerably more than the quarter of a million or so when IHT starts. If you are in that position get professional advice.

Do not try to avoid tax by giving away something but continuing to benefit from it. For example, if you give away your home but continue to live in it, the value of your home will still count as part of your estate even if the legal title actually belongs to someone else – such as one of your children.

Some insurance companies and financial consultants sell plans to reduce or avoid Inheritance Tax. Such schemes can be complicated – involving juggling the ownership of money or making gifts into or from trusts, and often involve taking out an insurance policy. These schemes are often designed to generate commission for the salesperson rather than benefit you. Before committing yourself to any scheme, be sure it has the approval of the Inland Revenue, and discuss it with an impartial professional adviser such as a solicitor or accountant. Generally they are best avoided.

For more information see Inland Revenue leaflets IHT3 *Inheritance Tax: an introduction*, IHT14 *Inheritance Tax: the personal representatives' responsibilities* and IHT15 *Inheritance Tax: how to calculate the liability* which are available from your tax office or the IR Capital Taxes Orderline on 0845 234 1000.

STAMP DUTY ON PROPERTY

When you buy a house or flat for more than £60,000, Stamp Duty will normally be due. The rates of Stamp Duty are:

Price of property	Rate of tax
Up to £60,000	nil
£60,001–£250,000	1% of total price
£250,001–£500,000	3% of total price
£500,001 and above	4% of total price

The Stamp Duty is due on the total price – so the tax on a home sold for £250,000 is 1 per cent, which equals £2,500, but the Stamp Duty due on a home sold for £250,001 is 3 per cent, which equals £7,505, an extra £5,005 tax on an extra £1 on the price! Stamp Duty is always rounded *up* to the next £5.

Tax-saving tip: If you are buying a home for just above £60,000, £250,000 or £500,000 try to negotiate with the owner to buy some fixtures and fittings separately to bring down the price to a lower tax band.

In some parts of the country designated as 'disadvantaged', the nil rate of Stamp Duty applies up to £150,000 not £60,000. You can find a complete list of the areas affected or do a postcode search to see if the property you are buying is in a 'disadvantaged' area on the Inland Revenue website at www.inlandrevenue.gov.uk/so/index.htm

Tax-saving tip: If you are buying a property for between £60,000 and £150,000 check its postcode to see if it is in a 'disadvantaged' area. You could save £1,500.

TAX ALLOWANCES AND RATES 2002–2003 AND 2003–2004

Allowances

	2002–2003	2003–2004
Personal Allowance		
Age		
Under 65	£4,615	£4,615
65 to 74 [1]	£6,100	£6,610
75 or more [1]	£6,370	£6,720
Blind Person's Allowance	£1,480	£1,510
Married Couple's Allowance [2]		
Age		
67 to 74 [3] [4]	£5,465	£5,565
75 or more [4]	£5,535	£5,635
Minimum amount	£2,110	£2,150
Income limit age-related allowances	£17,900	£18,300

Tax rates and bands

Tax bands – income above Personal Allowances		
Lower-rate tax applies to	First £1,920	First £1,960
Basic-rate tax applies to	£1,921 to £29,900	£1,961 to £30,500
Higher-rate tax applies to	Above £29,900	Above £30,500
Tax rates		
Lower rate	10%	10%
Basic rate – interest [5]	20%	20%
Basic rate – other income	22%	22%
Higher rate	40%	40%

NOTES

1   Allowance reduced by £1 for each £2 total income exceeds the income limit for age-related allowances, but never reduced below the level for those under 65.

2   The Married Couple's Allowance is not a true tax allowance. An amount equal to 10 per cent of it is deducted from the tax due.

3   Only available where the older partner was born before 6 April 1935.

4   Allowance reduced by £1 for each £2 by which total income exceeds an amount which has already reduced the Personal Allowance to its minimum amount. Allowance can never be reduced below the minimum amount.

5   Interest is always treated as the top slice of income when tax is being calculated.

Your Savings and Investments

This part of the book outlines the basic principles of saving and investment – and how to make your money work harder for you. As a nation we lose billions of pounds a year by not keeping an eye on our money. So here we explain the savings and investment choices you can make. We also look at how to make your everyday money, that sits in a bank account, work for you. We look at straightforward things like bank and building society accounts, National Savings, and ISAs, as well as more complicated investments such as individual shares, bonds, and unit and investment trusts. There is a checklist of factors you should consider before parting with your cash.

This section also tells you how to get financial advice and explains the new system of regulating financial advisers that will begin early in 2004. It also explains how to make a complaint about financial organisations – or get compensation if things go wrong.

We also take six people and show how they can save and make money by simple changes to their banking, saving and investing.

PRINCIPLES OF SAVING AND INVESTMENT

Savings are simply excess income. Or, to put it another way, money you don't spend. Whether these savings take the form of a lump sum in a building society account or used tenners stashed under your mattress is immaterial. If it is unspent income, it is savings. This book will help you make that money work harder for you. Left to itself money is a lazy creature – you have to put it to work and then you have to keep your eye on it to make sure there is no slacking. Interest rates change and best buys come and go. If you do not check on what your money is earning you will lose money.

Money-making tip: Check how much interest your money is earning (and how much interest any debt is incurring) at least once a year.

One way to set your money working is to invest it. But investment is very different from saving. When you invest money you give it temporarily to someone else so they can use it. They pay you for the privilege and say that they expect to return it to you at some time in the future. But you have to be careful. How much will they pay? Will they give it all back to you at the end? And even if they say they will give it back, can you enforce that promise? Generally, any investment puts your money at some risk – and despite what financial advisers may say to you – risk does not always mean reward; all too often it means loss.

Cash savings

Cash is the first thing any of us saves – we put money to one side for a holiday, for Christmas, for a new pair of shoes. Of course, nowadays people often do not do that – they borrow the money to buy what they want and then pay it back later. But all of us have saved up for something at some time, and however sophisticated our investment plans are, some of our savings will always be in cash – usually in a bank or building society account.

There are great advantages to cash:

- It remains your money and it is safe. Banks and building societies seldom collapse in the UK and even if one did, they all belong to a compensation scheme which protects most of your money up to £33,000 (see page 89 for details of compensation).
- It earns interest – or at least it should. Slowly your money will grow.
- It is accessible. You can take it back to spend at any time. Sometimes you will lose some of the interest it has earned if you take your money out without warning, but nowadays that is becoming rarer.
- All this means that if you put £10,000 into your savings account, you know that you can get at least £10,000 out, whenever you want it, in the future.

These advantages also lead to the big disadvantage of cash. Nothing exciting happens; your money does not grow very fast. And if you take the interest out as income as it is earned, you will only have left what you put in. Over the years that will be worth less and less. As prices rise, the buying power of this money falls. Over the last 20 years for example, prices have risen on average by 3.9 per cent a year. Since 1983 prices have more than doubled. So if you had £1,000 in 1983 you would need £2,159 now to buy as much as £1,000 would buy then. At that rate the value of money halves every 18 years. After five years £1,000 is worth £824 and it is worth only £680 after ten. So it is quite possible that if you put your money in a savings account the value of your savings will not keep pace with inflation.

Investments

Investment is the riskier side of saving. It means giving your money to someone else to use in the hope they can make it grow fast enough for them and you to see the advantage.

Some people see it as buying assets – such as shares. But in fact those assets are only worth what someone else will pay for them in the future. Your money is in limbo.

There are good reasons to invest. Over the last 100 years, money which has been invested in shares has grown faster than money kept in cash or money kept in 'fixed interest' investments such as bonds. If the past is a guide to the future, then investment will be a better way to wealth than saving. But there are problems:

- Your money is at risk. Some investments are safer than others, but ultimately they all depend on a company doing what you hope it will or a bank doing what it expects to do.
- Your money is inaccessible. To get your money back you will have to sell the investment to realise the cash. That will mean delays and, of course, costs. The selling price of something on a particular day is always less than the buying price, so if you invest it today you will get back less tomorrow even if the value of the investment has not changed. The value of investments does go up and down, so there are good and bad times to buy and sell them. You have to able to wait for – and spot – the good times.
- Part of your money will disappear every year. There will always be costs in any investment, partly to pay the salaries of the people who invest it and manage it. Some will make an upfront charge, taking maybe 5 per cent of your money just for the privilege of taking you on as a customer. Then there will be an annual management charge. Nowadays 1 per cent is typical but some kinds of investment will charge you a lot more.

Investment is also trickier than saving. The judgements you have to make in deciding where to invest your money, and how, are much more complicated than putting money in a bank account – and always remember that in the last 100 years there have been two periods of around 25 years when shares were worth no more at the end than at the start.

The tax cart

When you save or invest it is always sensible to think of the tax implications. However, saving or avoiding tax should never be the main reason for taking on a particular investment. Think of investing as a horse; it drives your finances forward. The tax you pay is the cart – the burden that the horse pulls. A light cart will never make a lame horse go fast. So never put the tax cart before the investment horse.

The Government encourages us to save for the future by offering tax advantages on the money we put into pensions and other sorts of savings and investments. Some deals from the Government do seem too good to miss. Every £78 we put into a pension is boosted by another £22 from the Chancellor. Cash ISAs accumulate interest free of tax. Some National Savings products grow without any tax being due. But before investing in any of them make sure the investment itself is what you need and is sound.

Husbands and wives can save tax by planning their investments together. If one pays no tax, or is taxed at a lower rate than the other, assets can be transferred to that partner. Always make sure, however, that you think about the implications of death, divorce, and bankruptcy.

You should always make sure that you are not paying too much tax on your investments. If you do nothing, tax at 20 per cent is automatically deducted from the interest earned on your savings. If you do not pay tax on your other income you can claim it back – or stop it happening. Remember that interest rates and returns are usually quoted before tax is deducted. If you have to pay tax, the actual return may be much less.

If you are thinking of retiring abroad, then tax becomes more important and complicated. You will normally be taxed only once on your money – in the country where you live no matter where the income arises. But there are complications and you must take care.

Finally, you should never make an investment just because there are tax advantages. In particular, you should never be persuaded by financial companies to take on a scheme because of tax savings. Make sure it is a good investment without the tax breaks as they can always be taken away by the Government in the future.

For further information, see Inland Revenue leaflet IR 110 *Bank and building society interest: A guide for savers.*

Things to consider

Pages 78–114 look in detail at the various different types of savings and investments that may be of interest to older people. No one investment or savings scheme is likely to meet all the priorities identified as part of your financial strategy. And in any case, the old saying that you should never put all your eggs in one basket applies even more to nest-eggs. So you will probably want to build up what is grandly called 'a portfolio' of different savings and investments.

On pages 118–136 we show how six people can save and make money by changing the way they save their money. The mix of savings and investments that is right for you will depend on your financial circumstances and, indeed, your personality. Because of this, you would be well advised to get some professional financial advice before parting with your money (see pages 71–77 for some tips on how to do this).

Whether or not you take advice, you should consider the points in the following checklist before deciding on a particular financial scheme.

Checklist

Before you invest in anything, ask if you should be investing at all. If you have debt, it may be better to use what spare money you have to pay that debt off. You will seldom earn more by investing £1,000 than you are being charged to borrow it. So pay off your credit card debt, get rid of the overdraft and see if you can pay off any bank loans early without being charged heavy penalties. Even paying off the mortgage may be more important than putting a bit of money into an ISA. Of course, few financial salespeople will tell you this; no-one earns commission when you pay off debt. But it is a vital question to ask yourself before you invest a penny.

If you do want to invest money, ask these questions – and keep the list with you when you go to see a financial adviser.

Risk Is your capital safe? If not, what is the worst that could happen? What has happened in the past? Is the same thing likely to happen in the future? Why?

Growth Does the scheme produce income or capital growth? If it provides income, how often is it paid? Is it guaranteed or is it variable? If it is guaranteed how is that achieved? Remember to take account of inflation and tax. If it provides capital growth, how long can that continue?

Access How long is your money tied up for? What is the notice period before you can cash in your investments? What is the cost of taking your money out? Is there a penalty for early withdrawal? Are there any limits on the amount you can take out?

Charges How much is the investment going to cost, whether it performs well or not? How much upfront? How much each year? What do you get for those charges? How much will the charges reduce the investment returns?

Protection Are you dealing with a reputable and authorised firm? Is it based in the UK? If not, who regulates it? How much of your money is protected by a compensation scheme if the company goes bust?

Taxation Is the scheme right for you from a tax point of view? If you are a non-taxpayer, is interest automatically paid with tax deducted? Will the income from the scheme mean that you pay a higher rate of tax? Beware of the age allowance trap (see page 15). What happens to your investment when you die?

PROTECTION FOR INVESTORS

The UK now has one of the most powerful financial regulators in the world. The Financial Services Authority (FSA) took on its full powers on 1 December 2001 and now regulates almost all the investment and savings products on the market as well as the people who sell them to us and the banks and financial companies that back them. It covers unit and investment trusts, pension schemes, endowment policies and futures and options.

Some investment and savings products are outside the scope of the FSA. They include National Savings products as well as current and savings accounts with banks and building societies. Also excluded are investments in physical things like property, stamps, precious stones, antiques, cars and wine. If you buy shares directly, including shares in an investment trust, you are not protected by the FSA. But if you buy the shares through an adviser or broker, they will be regulated and if they give you advice that too will be covered by the FSA. Mortgage advice and long-term care insurance will be regulated by the FSA from 31 October 2004 and general insurance from 14 January 2005.

The existence of the regulator does not mean that we do not have to be careful. Firms will still fail – the FSA itself has said that it does not operate a zero-failure regime. Crooks will still try to part us from our money. All investment will continue to carry some sort of risk. Nevertheless, having such a powerful regulator does help us be more confident that:

- people who sell us financial products are trained and registered;
- companies behind financial products are sound and trustworthy;
- advertisements for financial products are truthful and not misleading; and
- information about financial products is clear and straightforward.

The regulator cannot protect us against human weakness – greed can still drive both parties to a financial bargain and there will always be fools and knaves in financial institutions as elsewhere. If someone is determined to defraud investors, they will often succeed.

Getting financial advice

The way that financial advice is regulated will change early in 2004. Some of the principles will remain the same, however:

- A financial adviser will normally have to carry out a full interview with their client and establish what their investment aims and objectives are and judge which financial products best suit their needs.
- All individual financial advisers and the companies or networks they work for will have to be registered with the Financial Services Authority.
- All financial advisers will have to pass exams in financial products. There are various stages of these exams and some advisers will be better qualified than others. There are general exams and also specific ones in particular areas of financial planning such as pensions.

Important changes are planned for early 2004 in the organisation of most kinds of financial advice.

At the start of 2003–2004 financial advisers come in two sorts:

- **Independent financial advisers** have to survey the whole field of financial products from every company in the UK and offer the one that is most suitable to the client. They can be paid either by earning commission or by charging fees, or both.
- **Tied agents** represent one company and can only sell or discuss that company's products. However, tied agents working for some financial companies can sell stakeholder pensions from a small number of competitors.

Early in 2004, major changes are planned in the way that financial advisers work. Under the plans, there will probably be three sorts of financial adviser, but it will be hard to tell them apart:

- **Independent financial advisers** who have to survey the whole field of financial products from every company in the UK and offer the one that is most suitable to the client. They will have to offer you the opportunity to pay a fee rather than earning commission. But as long as they explain their charges clearly, customers will be able to choose to pay them through commission rather than a fee.
- **Financial advisers – who do not call themselves 'independent'** – will be able to sell products from a more limited range of companies and can work on commission or on fees as they choose.
- **Financial advisers who are employed by one bank or finance company** will in future be able to sell their own company's products alongside products from a range of competitor companies.

The FSA is also discussing a further split of advisers in all three categories into two tiers – an upper tier of fully qualified advisers who advise across the whole range of products and a lower tier of advisers with more limited training who advise on a limited range of simpler products. The latter may not have an obligation to carry out a full financial review with every client.

Independent financial advisers

If you want financial advice, you should always use an independent financial adviser (IFA). The word 'independent' means that they are obliged by law to find you the best deal for your circumstances. Of course, some IFAs are better than others. But financial advisers who are not independent are not worth even considering because they are limited by law in what they can tell you and sell you.

Today, most IFAs will earn their money by taking commission on the final sale. If they sell you nothing, they earn nothing. How much they earn depends in part on what they sell you – some products are far more profitable than others. Under the law, the commission they might earn plays no part in the advice IFAs give.

But human nature being what it is, customers certainly feel it does and few IFAs would claim it never plays a part.

For this reason a growing number of IFAs do not take commission. Instead they charge their customers a fee. However, commission is so deep-seated in the financial services industry that it is still paid by the company selling the product, so the IFA has to give it back to the customer, either in cash or by increasing the size of their investment. Some IFAs will work on either basis – commission or fees.

Even IFAs who charge fees will give you one free session to see if both sides think it is worth pursuing matters. Once you get into paid time, £100 an hour is at the lower end. You will pay more in cities and wealthier parts of the UK. The fee will have to be paid whether you buy a product or not.

It is illegal for anyone to offer most financial advice or to provide access to investment products without being registered to do so. If you buy products from a person or company who is not registered, then you are not covered by the protection and compensation schemes that exist. You can check if a person or company is registered with the FSA by phoning the number on page 167 or through its website at www.fsa.gov.uk

You can get a list of IFAs in your local area from the internet on www.ifap.org.uk or www.sofa.org or www.searchifa.co.uk or you can ring IFA Promotions hotline at the number on page 167. But the best way to find a financial adviser is by a personal recommendation from a friend who has one they trust who has done well for them over a period of time.

You should always insist that your first visit to an IFA is at their office. It is more businesslike and you are more in control than if they come to your home. Try out two or three – remember the first interview is free – and see if you like them and find what they say sensible. Remember to ask the difficult questions, such as:

- What experience and qualifications does your adviser have?
- Does your adviser or the firm specialise in any particular areas, such as pensions or advice for the over-50s?

- How many clients does each adviser deal with? (If the answer is more than 400, can you be sure that you will get the attention you should?)
- How does the firm keep up to date with new products and developments? What computer backup does it have?

It is also a good idea to ask to speak to some of the firm's existing clients. If the adviser will not put you in touch with other customers, then walk away. Other clients should be able to give you an inside view on the sort of service you can expect. If you don't like the answers you get or the attitude of the adviser, walk away. Finance is a very personal business and it is essential that you like and trust the people you deal with.

When an adviser recommends a particular investment, you should ask more questions. Ask:

- Why is it right for me?
- Could I lose money?
- What are the alternatives?
- What will I get out of the deal?

Bear in mind the following points too:

- Be suspicious of any promise of exceptional returns: if a deal sounds too good to be true, it probably is.
- Never be bamboozled into investing in a scheme you don't understand – particularly if your adviser is vague about the details or does not seem to understand it themselves.
- Don't be panicked into parting with your money because your adviser says that you must take advantage of a special offer immediately.
- Alarm bells should ring if you are told to cash in all your investments so that the adviser can invest them elsewhere – he or she may be recycling investments unnecessarily in order to boost commission. This process, known as 'churning', is not legal but is not uncommon either.
- Be very suspicious of an adviser who tells you to put all your money into one investment. That breaks the key rule of investment which is to spread your risk.

- Never make a cheque payable to an individual in a firm of financial advisers. Make out your cheque to the firm in which your money is to be invested.
- Keep up to date by reading the financial sections of newspapers and magazines and listening to programmes such as *Money Box* on Radio 4 and *Working Lunch* on BBC TWO.

The FSA publishes a free booklet, *Guide to financial advice*, which gives more tips on avoiding bad investments. The FSA's address is on page 167.

Regulations affecting financial advisers

Advisers selling regulated financial products have to follow certain procedures.

Disclosure of commission They have to tell you how much commission the salesperson is getting. Companies that do not pay sales-based commission to staff must provide a comparable quote that takes account of a range of factors including a proportion of the salesperson's basic salary, the cost of training the salesperson, the cost of equipment required by the salesperson and the cost of the premises and support staff to provide the sales service. However, commission disclosure is not normally early enough, or often clear enough, to help you in your decision. It is supposed to be improved in 2004 as part of the changes to financial advice.

Key features Advisers are also required to advise you of the product's 'key features'. In other words, they must tell you about its aims, risks and benefits, as well as the impact of charges and expenses. A personal illustration must also be given, showing projected costs and fund growth based on the customer's personal circumstances.

'Reason why' The adviser must also provide you with a 'reason why' letter explaining why the product is right for you.

Cooling off You normally have a period in which you can cancel the deal without penalty. You must be told clearly what this cooling off period is.

Complaining

If you believe that you have been sold a wrong or inappropriate investment, or that a financial firm has been negligent, incompetent or downright dishonest, there is a set procedure for complaining which all registered financial firms have to follow.

First, you should write to the Chief Executive of the company setting out clearly your complaint and what you want to be done about it. If that does not produce the result you want, or if your complaint is not dealt with to your satisfaction within eight weeks, your case has reached what is called 'deadlock' and you can go to the Financial Ombudsman Service.

Ombudsman

You can complain to the Financial Ombudsman about any financial firm, such as a bank or investment company, which is registered with the FSA. For example, you may have been sold the wrong product, or sold something without the risks being explained. Or you may just feel that your bank has mishandled your instructions over a direct debit or standing order. The Ombudsman can deal with complaints about any company registered with the FSA even if the complaint concerns a product – such as a current account – which is itself not regulated by the FSA. You have six months from the time your case is 'deadlocked' to go to the Financial Ombudsman.

In many cases the Ombudsman will resolve the problem quickly by finding a compromise acceptable to both sides. If that is not possible then the case proceeds to a formal investigation and a preliminary decision. Normally, the company will accept that. If it does not, it can appeal to the Chief Ombudsman. Once the Chief Ombudsman gives a formal ruling, which can include compensation to the customer, the company has to follow it. There is no direct appeal to the courts, although some companies have tried to get the courts to overturn the Ombudsman's decisions.

The Financial Ombudsman Service is free. You do not need a lawyer to argue your case, although if you want professional help you will have to pay for it. There is a new breed of company calling themselves 'claims handlers' who will offer to take you through the process in return for a hefty slice of any compensation. They are generally not a good idea. If you disagree with the ruling or the compensation ordered then you can still go to court, although that is likely to be stressful, expensive and time-consuming.

Further information is available from the Ombudsman at the address on page 167.

When compensation is paid

Sometimes a financial company goes out of business, leaving investors out of pocket or insurance claims unmet. There is one Financial Services Compensation Scheme (FSCS) with one set of rules which sorts out compensation in all these cases. The maximum amounts of compensation do vary, however, from one sort of investment to another. If you lose money which is on deposit in a bank or building society, you can now get up to £31,700 in compensation – on a joint account each partner can get this amount. The maximum for a claim on an insurance policy that is not met by the insurer is 100 per cent of the first £2,000 and 90 per cent of the rest. If an investment company goes bust, the maximum compensation is £48,000. You normally have to ask for compensation within six years of the company going out of business.

This scheme only applies to firms which are regulated by the FSA. If you invest in a company based in another country, even if the product was sold to you in the UK, you will have to rely on the compensation scheme in that country.

You can find out more about the Financial Services Compensation Scheme from the address on page 167.

BANK AND BUILDING SOCIETY ACCOUNTS

The distinction between banks and building societies is almost disappearing. Many familiar building societies have become banks or been bought by a bank and they all offer similar accounts and products. The only difference is that with a building society, all the profits are ploughed back into the society; with a bank, some of the profits are distributed to shareholders. That should mean building societies offer a better deal, but it does not always work like that.

Current accounts

Nowadays, all your cash – even if it is in a current account – should be earning money. The main high street banks will pay you virtually nothing on your current account: rates of 0.1 per cent are normal. That means that £1,000 sitting there all year would bring in just £1 at the end of the year, and that would be before deducting 20p tax.

There are now many accounts where you will get paid a more reasonable rate of interest on your current account balance. The best rates are paid on accounts which are run over the Internet or using the phone. You can get 3 per cent or more at the time of writing – that means £1,000 would bring you in £30 (before tax) at the end of the year. There is more information on internet banking on page 81. Many of us of course prefer to use a bank where we can visit a branch and see someone face to face. But even here there are now banks or building societies with branches where you can earn 3 per cent on your current account.

Money-making tip: If your bank or building society does not pay interest on your current account, move it to one that does.

Since 1 January 2002 it has been a lot easier to move your current account. Your old bank has to tell your new bank about all your standing orders and direct debits within five days and co-operate fully in your move to the new bank. It can take three or four weeks to get it all sorted out, but can be well worth it.

Of course, a current account is not just about interest. It is about standing orders, cash dispensers, charges, overdrafts, how quickly money is credited to your account and how easy it is to change and sort out your financial affairs. So you have to choose an account to suit you.

Just about all banks now belong to the Link cash machine network and you can withdraw money without paying a charge from any bank's Link machine – although some Link machines in small supermarkets and shops, garages, motorway service areas and even some post offices will make a charge which will be shown on the screen before you take out your money.

When money is paid into an account – or taken out – it goes through what is called the 'clearing system'. Banks in the clearing system should take three days between the money leaving one account to its being credited in the other, although some take longer, especially if you pay in a cheque. Some of the newer banks are not in the clearing system. With them, it can take up to ten days after you have paid the money in before you can get hold of it.

Overdraft interest rates are very high. With some banks you can still be charged interest of around 20 per cent even on an overdraft you have agreed with the bank. If you go overdrawn without having an arrangement, expect to pay up to 30 per cent. In addition, banks may make one-off charges for recording the overdraft, writing you a letter about it, or stopping a cheque or automatic payment.

If you think you may go overdrawn on your account, remember that overdraft rates vary enormously and some banks now offer rates as low as 9 per cent and many will allow you to overdraw by a small amount – up to £250 in some cases – free of charge. *MoneyFacts* supplies details of overdraft terms as part of its information service (see page 171).

Money-saving tip: If you think you will need to make use of an overdraft regularly, you should pick an account with a low interest rate on agreed overdrafts and keep below the agreed limit.

Although banks have been closing branches for many years, some now allow you to use your local post office to pay money in and out and pay bills, all free of charge, although there may be an extra delay before money is credited to your account.

Nowadays, some of the best savings deals are with the banks not the building societies. But if you are a long-standing member of a society and you think that it may convert to a bank, you should keep your account open with a small amount of money in case you are in line for a windfall.

Savings accounts

The distinction between savings accounts and current accounts gets less all the time (there are internet current accounts that offer better rates of interest than almost any savings account). There is a bewildering array of savings accounts from banks and building societies but it is not hard to work out which is best for you.

The first and most important thing to look at is the rate of interest which will be paid on the money you want to save. After all, it is about money and how much you make – you can get twice as much with the best as with the worst.

Second, you have to consider when you want the interest paid. If you want a regular income from your savings then you will want your interest credited every month or perhaps every quarter. But if you just want the money to grow and do not need to spend the income, then choose an account with an annual rate of interest. Interest paid monthly is always slightly less in total than annual interest on the same account because you have had the money earlier.

Third, will you operate your account exclusively over the Internet? Normally you will get better rates of interest that way.

Fourth, how long do you want your money tied up for? In the past, the longer you tied up your money or the more you had to save, the higher the rate of interest you could earn. Not any more. You can get top rates on savings for amounts of £1 with instant access to your cash without penalties, although to get the very best rates you have to be willing to operate the account through the Internet. If you cannot do that, then you can sneak a few fractions of per cent more by tying up your money for three months or even three years. But there is not much in it.

Finally, remember that the interest you earn on current or savings accounts has 20 per cent tax deducted from it automatically. If your total annual income is below about £8,570 then you should probably only pay tax at 10 per cent and you can claim back the excess tax. If your total annual income is below about £6,600 then you should pay no tax and you can claim back the tax that has been taken off you and register to have your interest paid gross without tax being deducted in future. These figures apply to people aged 65 or more and are slightly higher if you are over 75. For more details on tax on savings see pages 10–14.

Internet banking

If you have a computer and an internet connection then you can get the best deals for your money by moving your bank or building society accounts to an internet only account. Many people are afraid of using the Internet in this way. But you should not be. Internet accounts, as far as anyone knows, are completely safe and secure.

One big advantage is that interest rates are generally higher and overdraft rates generally lower. There are two reasons for that. First, the banks save money because they do not have to keep branches open and pay staff, nor do they post you out statements. Second, they are trying to attract new customers, so they offer the top deals to them. Most internet banks are still running at a loss – that means the bank is losing and you are winning. But do not worry about them going out of business as almost all are subsidiaries of major banks; stick with one of those and you are fully protected.

Internet accounts also put you much more in charge of your money. You can look at your account, move money around, check your balance, and see what payments have come in and gone out 24 hours a day 365 days a year. If you have any queries about your account or want to change the way you pay bills, you can do it all over the computer, although almost all of them have a telephone helpline as well if you get stuck.

Of course, there are some disadvantages. Many people like the personal service of calling in to their local branch if they have one. You also need a modern up-to-date computer at home. It needs to be a fairly new one or it will not have the necessary security to operate the account. You will also have to be connected to the Internet and pay the costs of that. You will not be sent bank statements – they can be seen online but you should always print out a copy for yourself once a month in case there are queries. Some internet banks do not let you have a chequebook – so all payments have to be done electronically through the computer. Remember too that even though the money will leave your account immediately, it will still take three or four days to reach another bank.

Money-saving tip: If you haven't tried internet banking, why not open an account and put a bit of money in it to see how easy it is? If you like it, then you can think of transferring all your money to cyberspace.

Offshore accounts

Most UK banks offer what they call 'offshore' savings accounts. These are usually at branches or subsidiaries located in the Channel Islands or the Isle of Man and offer reasonable rates of interest with the advantage that the interest is credited gross, without tax being deducted. Of course, if you are a taxpayer you still have to pay tax on it, and you will do that through a self-assessment form. If you do not already get a self-assessment form, then there is little point to putting money offshore. But if you pay higher-rate tax, or already get self-assessed for some other reason, then it does defer the tax you have to pay for a little while. However, unless you have quite a lot of money to spare it is probably not worthwhile.

If there is more than £5,000 in an offshore account, some delay may occur after death before probate is granted (ie before the Will is approved and the dead person's assets released). If it is a joint account, the surviving partner should send a copy of the death certificate to the bank or building society. The assets of the joint account will then be registered in the survivor's name. There is no charge for this service.

Protection

Very very occasionally, a UK bank goes bust. If it does, then any money in an account is protected by the Financial Services Compensation Scheme. You will get the first £2,000 in full and then 90 per cent of the next £33,000. (See page 77 for more details of the compensation scheme.)

Cash ISAs

Individual Savings Accounts (ISAs) replaced TESSAs and PEPs for all investments made after 5 April 1999. There are two quite separate types of ISA – a cash ISA, which is a savings account where you can invest cash, and an investment ISA, where the money will normally be at risk on the stock market. Confusingly, both are called ISAs. This section deals with cash ISAs. Investment ISAs are dealt with on pages 110–111. If you want to invest into an investment ISA, that may affect the amount of money you can invest in a cash ISA or who you invest it with.

Each tax year you can put up to £3,000 into a cash ISA (also called a mini-cash ISA), which is really just a savings account on which interest is paid. An ISA account has two big advantages:

- The interest is free of tax. It is credited to the account gross and there is no tax to pay – you do not even have to tell the Inland Revenue about it.
- Interest rates tend to be slightly higher than for other investment accounts. So even if you are a non-taxpayer a cash ISA may be a good idea.

The best cash ISAs have a 'CAT' mark. This is a government standard which stands for 'Costs, Access, Terms' and means that the charges are low and the conditions are fair. To qualify for this standard you must be able to get your cash within seven days, pay into the account amounts as small as £10, and the interest paid must be within two points of the Bank of England base rate.

You can take your money out of an ISA at any time without a penalty and still keep the tax relief on the interest it has earned. The only restriction is that you cannot pay in more than £3,000 in total during the tax year. So if you put in the maximum £3,000 in April, you can take out £1,000 in November, for example, but cannot put any more in until the next April. However, if you only put in £2,000 in April and take out £1,000 in November you can put another £1,000 back in.

Some cash ISAs are not CAT marked because they insist that you invest more than £10 – for example the whole of your annual limit of £3,000 – or they impose restrictions on when you can take the money out. These non-CAT-marked ISAs can be suitable and can offer the best deal. But make sure that you understand the restrictions fully.

Money-making tip: If you have some money on deposit and you are a taxpayer, put it into an instant access, CAT-marked ISA. The interest will be tax-free and you can take the money out at any time.

TESSAs

Cash ISAs replaced the old Tax Exempt Special Savings Accounts (TESSAs) and are much more flexible. With a TESSA you had to wait until it matured after five years before you could take the money out and keep the tax relief on the interest it had earned. The last date for starting a TESSA was 5 April 1999 and as they took five years to 'mature' they will still be with us until April 2004.

There are special rules for maturing TESSAs – the money you invested in the TESSA (which is up to £9,000) can be put straight into a special cash ISA on top of the normal ISA limit. You cannot transfer the interest the TESSA has earned, only the money you put into it. These investments are called follow-on TESSAs or TESSA Only ISAs – usually known as TOISAs for short.

The interest rates you can get on TOISAs vary widely so it is essential to shop around. The best source of impartial advice on them is *MoneyFacts* (see page 171).

If you still have a TESSA, remember that you can put up to £1,800 into it each year as long as the total you have invested does not exceed £9,000. All interest earned is tax-free. If the interest is withdrawn it is paid net of 20 per cent tax and that amount is retained in the TESSA until the end of the five-year period. If any capital is withdrawn, the tax exemption is lost and the account becomes a normal deposit account.

Fixed rate accounts

All the accounts mentioned so far have a variable rate of interest – in other words as interest rates rise and fall, the rate you are paid on your money will rise and fall too. The bank base rate stayed steady at 4 per cent from November 2001 to January 2003. But in February 2003 it fell to 3.75 per cent and it may fall again in future. Savings accounts have followed suit, and more, and most pay less now than they did a year or so ago. Fixed rate accounts are different. They guarantee you at the outset that your money will pay a fixed return for a fixed period of, for example, 4 per cent over two years. You have to agree to leave your money in for that length of time. You can receive the interest at the end or annually. Some cash ISAs are fixed rate and promise a fixed return over a fixed period. These products are sometimes called 'term accounts' or 'fixed rate bonds' – but beware because the word 'bond' can apply to many sorts of investment; some like these which are safe, but also to others which are very risky.

There are two advantages to fixed rate accounts:

- When interest rates are low, you may well be offered more than the current rate. At the time of writing, you would be lucky to get even 4 per cent on your savings, but one bond was offering 4.5 per cent over three years on £500.
- You know exactly what your income will be even if interest rates change.

And three drawbacks:

- You have to invest a minimum amount – usually £1,000 or more.
- Your money is tied up for the period of the term. If you take it out before the end you will pay a financial penalty.
- If interest rates generally rise, you may end up with a poor return.

In other words you are gambling about future interest rates. If they fall, you win the gamble; if they rise you lose.

Guaranteed income bonds

Another sort of investment which uses the word 'bond' is also completely safe, even though it is sold by insurance companies rather than banks or building societies. Guaranteed income bonds are as safe as a deposit account. You need at least £5,000 to invest and your money is tied up for a period which ranges from one to five years. The returns do not look spectacular – but they are paid after basic-rate tax has been deducted. Non-taxpayers cannot recover it and higher-rate taxpayers will have more to pay. They are only suitable if you pay basic rate or higher rate tax. You can get more than 3 per cent on a three year bond, which is equivalent to about 4 per cent gross. The more you invest, and the longer it is tied up for, the higher the return. The money earned can be paid monthly or annually. Some bonds pay at the end of the investment and are then called guaranteed growth bonds.

NATIONAL SAVINGS & INVESTMENTS

The Government backs National Savings & Investments (the new name for National Savings) and so all its products are as close as you can get to an absolute guarantee that your money is safe. You can get income, capital growth, protection from inflation, or, of course, take a gamble with premium bonds. There are two other advantages with National Savings & Investments products – some pay out tax-free and so are good for taxpayers, especially if you pay higher-rate tax. Others pay the interest gross and so non-taxpayers do not have to worry about reclaiming tax that has been automatically deducted, and taxpayers keep their money until they sort out their tax at the end of the year.

Savings certificates

If you want tax-free capital growth over a fixed period of two or five years with complete safety then National Savings Certificates may suit you. If you cash the certificate in early you will be charged a stiff penalty. Even if you keep them for the full term the rate of interest is not great, but for higher-rate taxpayers they may be better than other returns after 40 per cent tax has been paid. At the end of the period you will be asked what you want to do with your money. If you do not respond it will be reinvested for you in a similar product and may well be tied up for some time.

Some certificates are 'index-linked'. This means that they pay an interest rate which is a fixed amount above the rate of inflation. Index-linked certificates are particularly attractive if you think inflation is going to rise.

You can invest anything between £100 and £10,000 into certificates.

Capital bonds

For guaranteed growth over one, three or five years, capital and fixed rate bonds can give reasonable value. The interest is paid gross each year but it is taxable. You need at least £500 to invest but can invest up to £1 million in total in National Savings bonds. You should avoid cashing in the bond early as you will suffer hefty penalties.

Income and pensioner bonds

If you are 60 or more, you can get a regular monthly income and a reasonable rate of interest from pensioner bonds. Income bonds are similar for younger people. You need at least £500 to invest (the maximum is £1 million). The rate of interest is guaranteed for one, two or five years. Of course you run the risk that interest rates will rise and you will be stuck with a bad rate. On the other hand, if interest rates fall further, people who took them out in the past will seem to have a very good deal. There are tough penalties for cashing in early.

Children's Bonus Bond

These bonds for children under 16 are usually taken out as five-year savings plans by grandparents or other relatives. The interest received is free of all tax and offers a guaranteed annual return over five years. They come in £25 units and the maximum you can buy is £1,000 worth.

Premium bonds

The rate of return of premium bonds is not good (2.25 per cent at time of writing) but the prizes are tax-free and there is always that small chance of winning £1 million – the odds are much better than the National Lottery. You need to buy at least £100 and can buy up to £20,000 worth. Higher-rate taxpayers may find them attractive – 300,000 savers have the maximum holding.

Guaranteed equity bonds

Money invested in National Savings & Investments guaranteed equity bonds will grow for five years in line with the FTSE 100 index of shares in our biggest hundred companies. If the index falls over that period then you will get your original investment back in full. There are no fees or charges. Your money is tied up for five years. So the risk you run is that the stock market falls or rises very little over that time and your money would have done better on deposit. The bonds are not always available. If you are interested you can register to be told of the next issue on a form from the Post Office or through the National Savings & Investments website.

Other products

National Savings & Investments also offers a cash ISA which has a reasonable rate of interest, although you can do better elsewhere. Both its current account and its savings account offer poor returns. The first £70 of interest a year earned on the ordinary account is tax-free, but the rate of interest is so low that you would only earn half that much in a year even on the maximum balance of £10,000. Your money is better elsewhere.

You can get the *Investors' guide* and other free National Savings & Investments leaflets from 0845 964 5000 or some post offices. The National Savings & Investments website at www.nsandi.com has a lot of useful information.

GOVERNMENT STOCK (GILTS)

Lending directly to the Government is probably the safest way to invest your money. You do it by buying government stock, generally known as 'gilt-edged securities' or 'gilts'. You lend your money to the Government and it guarantees to give you all your money back at a certain time and meanwhile pays you interest at a fixed rate. The interest is paid in two instalments each year. It is taxable but is normally paid gross and you will have to pay the tax through self-assessment.

The Government sells gilts in certificates with what is called a 'nominal' value of £100. The certificate contains a 'redemption date', which is the date on which the holder will be repaid £100 for it, and a 'coupon', which is the name for the rate of interest paid on that £100 each year.

For example, 7¾ per cent Treasury stock 2006 promises to pay the holder of a £100 certificate £7.75 a year in two instalments on 8 March and 8 September and redeem the certificates by repaying the £100 on 8 September 2006.

These particular certificates were first issued in May 1993 when interest rates were 6 per cent and most people were anticipating rates would rise. Today, earning 7¾ per cent on your money even for the next three years is very attractive and people who bought them then have done very well. You can still buy this stock. But to get a £100 certificate you would have to pay more than £100. If you bought it for £113.25, for example, you would still get £7.75 a year, paid in two instalments which is a return on your £113.25 of around 6.5 per cent.

It still sounds attractive, and is certainly more than you can currently earn on your money in a deposit account. But you also have to take account of what happens when the stock reaches its redemption date. When September 2006 arrives you would only get back £100 for an outlay of £113.25. So you have lost £13.25. And that must be taken off your interest payments over the time you held it. Once you have taken account of the fact that money now is worth more than money tomorrow, you arrive at what is called a 'redemption yield', which is a measure of the real overall return on your money. The arithmetic is complex but in this example it would be around 3.7 per cent. In this way, the market ensures that the price of gilts reflects their value in the light of expectations about interest rates. The *Financial Times* publishes lists of all government stock each day, together with their yields.

If a gilt is paying a coupon that is low, then you may be able to buy it for less than £100. At redemption you would make a capital gain. However, that gain is free of tax and is not counted as part of your overall capital gains. Similarly, any capital loss cannot be offset against your capital gains in other areas. (For more on Capital Gains Tax see pages 53–56.) If you are a higher-rate taxpayer, you may be better off with a low-coupon stock, bought for less than £100, which means you get less income which is taxed and get a capital gain which is tax-free at redemption. However, with interest rates at their current low level, there are almost no gilts that are being sold for less than £100.

Gilts can also be attractive for people looking for a regular monthly income. Although most gilts pay interest only twice a year, you can build up a portfolio of six different gilts, paying in different months, to secure an income each month.

Some gilts have more than one date – such as 5½ per cent Treasury Stock 2008–2012. That means that the Government (not the investor) decides when to redeem it between those two dates.

A more complicated product is index-linked stock. Here the interest rate or coupon is lower (typically 2½ per cent) but both the interest payments and the final value of the stock is index linked. In other words each year you get more than £2.50, and at its redemption date you get £100 plus inflation for each £100 certificate. As a result, the market value of these gilts is considerably more than £100.

Some stocks have no date for redemption. With these stocks the Government can choose when – and indeed if – it will redeem the capital. There is a group of 'rump' stocks in which there is no market – if you hold one of these you are stuck with it.

You can buy and sell gilts through banks, some building societies, stockbrokers and also by post on a form available at post offices.

You can get the form from the Bank of England by ringing 0800 818 614 or from its website at www.bankofengland.co.uk/registrars/brokeragehome.htm Further information is available by writing to the Bank of England Registrar's Department or by ringing the Bank on 01452 398333.

The commission you pay on small transactions of stock may be less when you deal direct with the Bank of England by post than through a broker or bank, but for larger transactions it may be cheaper through a broker. Either way the commission has also to be taken into account when working out the yield on your money.

Using the postal dealing service you pay 0.7 per cent on the first £5,000, subject to a minimum of £12.50 for purchases (no minimum commission for sales), and £35 plus 0.375 per cent on any amount over £5,000. So you would pay £12.50 commission if you invested £1,000, £35 commission for £5,000 invested, and £53.75 for £10,000. On sales, you would pay, for example, only £1.75 commission on proceeds of £250, £17.50 on £2,500, and £44.38 on £7,500.

The main disadvantage of using the postal dealing service is that there will be a delay between you signing your cheque and the money being invested. If gilt prices change in the meantime, you may end up getting less (or more) for your money than you were expecting.

You can find out more about gilts from the Debt Management Office (see address on page 166) which administers them for the Government and which produces a free booklet called *Investing in gilts: the private investor's guide to British Government stock* which contains a lot of information about gilts and how they work. You can get a copy from the Bank of England by ringing 0800 818 614, or you can get more information from the DMO website at www.dmo.gov.uk where you can download a copy of the guide.

Local authority bonds

A few local councils raise money by issuing bonds. They offer a fixed rate of interest which will not change over a fixed period of between one and six years. You normally have to invest at least £500 and interest is paid twice a year.

INVESTING IN COMPANIES

Shares

For most people, investment implies buying shares in companies – ie investing in the stock market. From 1975 to 1999 the value of shares went up consistently and putting your money in shares seemed a one-way bet to wealth. But from the start of 2000 shares fell. People have learned the hard way the truth of the warning that the value of shares can go down as well as up. The overall price of shares in London fell by 10 per cent in 2000 and then by another 16 per cent in 2001 and again by 25 per cent in 2002. In the three years from the peak at the start of the millennium to the end of 2002, the value of shares in our biggest hundred companies fell by almost half. It is a sobering thought that over the last 100 years shares have fallen in four years out of ten. Nevertheless, most financial advisers will say that investing in shares still has an important part to play in any long-term investment strategy.

A share is literally a share in the ownership of the company. Put simply, if the company is worth £1 billion and you own one share of £1 you own a billionth of the company. There are two parts to the return you may get on a share:

- **Capital gains:** The value of the share may rise. That means you can sell your share for more than you paid for it and make a profit – technically you make a capital gain and, as long as your gains in the year are less than £7,900, you pay no tax on that. Of course, over the last three years the chances are that the value of your shares has fallen, so if you sold them you would get less than you paid for them. But that loss is only made when you sell the shares – if you hang on and share prices rise, then you may find that the losses are reversed.
- **Income:** The company may pay you a dividend (ie a share of the profit the company has made). If the company make profits of £100 million and there are a billion shares in issue, then for each share you may get given a dividend of

10p. Such a return would be rare, however. Firstly, many companies do not currently make significant profits. Secondly, those that do, often want to reinvest them rather than give them to shareholders. The result is that the return on investments in the stock market is typically around 3.75 per cent a year. In other words if you buy shares worth £1,000, the dividends you get will be around £37.50 in the course of the year. That money is taxable and is paid with 10 per cent tax already deducted. (For more on how dividends are taxed see page 13.)

The price of a share in a particular company depends on many factors. These factors include sensible things like the amount of profit the company makes, its plans for the future, the ability of its management team, and the prospects for that type of business. But the price will also be affected by other less rational factors. For example, a belief that the share price will rise can itself cause it to rise as people buy shares hoping to make a quick buck. Towards the end of 1999 and in early 2000 people believed that shares in technology and communications companies could only rise. It was only in March 2000 that everyone realised these companies seldom made a profit and many had huge debts. Share prices plummeted. Some companies went bust and the shares in the others have still not recovered. If a company is a take-over target, then the share price will rise as investors buy up shares believing that they will be offered a good price by the company that wants to buy it. If a company faces bankruptcy, then the shares will become valueless and your investment will be worthless. Sometimes the value of shares goes down for no apparent reason – dealers in the City are said to have 'lost confidence' in the firm or its managers. A sell-off follows and the price falls sharply.

Indices

You will often hear rises and falls in UK share prices reported on radio and TV or even in the newspapers as a movement in 'The Footsie'. That usually means the FTSE 100 index, which is produced by the *Financial Times* and the London Stock

Exchange, and which measures the movement in the value of shares in the biggest hundred companies on the Exchange. The FTSE 100 is weighted so that the changes in the value of shares in the biggest companies has a bigger effect on the index than changes in smaller companies. This index rises and falls each moment the stock market is open as the prices of shares changes.

Another index is the FTSE All Share index. Contrary to its name, it is not all the shares listed on the London Stock Exchange but only the 750 or so which are actively traded. There is also the FTSE TechMark index, which measures the changes in price of shares of technology and communications companies.

Each stock market has its own indices. The Dow Jones Industrial Average ('The Dow') is an index of just 30 typical large companies on the New York Stock Exchange, excluding those in transport or utilities. There is another stock market in the United States of America known as the 'Nasdaq'. It is an electronic stock exchange and the Nasdaq Composite Index measures the movement in the shares in more than 5,000 companies which trade on it. In Japan, the Nikkei Stock Average takes 225 representative and actively traded shares on the Tokyo Stock Exchange.

Corporate bonds

There are other ways to invest in the fortunes of a company apart from buying shares. A corporate bond is a loan to a company in exchange for which it gives you a fixed and guaranteed rate of interest and a promise to give you back your capital at the end of a fixed period. There is less risk than with shares, as the value of the investment remains the same and interest is guaranteed. But there is still a risk – the company may go bust and default on its payments. Generally, the riskier the company the higher the return on your money. But also the greater the risk you will not get it back.

You can minimise this risk by investing in a fund which holds corporate bonds in a range of companies. These are done through unit trusts (see pages 103–104). However, as investors' confidence in shares declines, many advisers try to sell other investments as 'less risky'. Corporate bonds may be less risky than shares but they are by no means safe.

Investment bonds

These are single-premium life insurance policies, the money from which is invested by the life insurance companies in a separate fund of pooled investments, rather like a unit trust. Thus indirectly your money is invested in companies.

The attraction of these bonds is the tax-deferred income they provide. This can be particularly useful for older people who need to keep their tax bill down to qualify for the higher age-related Personal Allowances (see pages 15–16 for details). Individuals can withdraw up to 5 per cent of their original investment from the bond each year for up to 20 years as tax-deferred income. The 5 per cent is cumulative, so if you don't use it one year, you can add it to the next year's allowance. Higher-rate taxpayers may be liable to tax, at a rate which equals the difference between the basic and higher rate, on any profits made. Investment advisers can provide clients with a list of capital-protected bonds.

Equity income bonds

These products are marketed under a variety of names, such as 'high-income' or 'equity income' bonds, and are sold by some well-known high street names. But they are dangerous and should be avoided. The return on your capital is linked to stock market performance. The bonds 'guarantee' you a return on your investment of 7 per cent or more a year for a fixed period of time. Generally they will pay you the return promised each year – so in that sense the income is 'guaranteed'. But the return of your capital is not. That depends on stock market performance and when markets fall, as they have recently, you will lose some, most, or even all of your original investment. One way to look at it is that you have been paid your income by running down your capital. They are best avoided.

Friendly societies

Another way of investing in the stock market is through a friendly society. They were begun along with building societies more than 200 years ago as self-help organisations, sometimes to help people save up for their own funeral. They still provide a tax-free way to save up small amounts over ten years. They are often used by parents and grandparents who want to invest on behalf of children – perhaps for university costs or a wedding – but they can also be used to save up for a car or a holiday for example.

The ten-year savings schemes come with some life insurance cover (which you may not need) and because they are tax-free, they are of most use for higher-rate taxpayers, or for basic-rate taxpayers edging over the age allowance limit (see page 15). The most you can pay in is £270 a year or £25 a month. Plans must be held for ten years for maximum benefit and there are penalties for early surrender. The life cover varies depending on sex and age at entry. A surrender value is paid if the policy has been in force for more than one year and all premiums for the first year have been paid. A guaranteed sum assured is payable on death provided policy conditions are met.

Despite their name, charges levied by these societies are anything but friendly. Many smaller societies do not benefit from the economies available to larger organisations. Check also that the quoted rates of return are as good as the best from banks, building societies and National Savings & Investments. The Friendly Societies Protection Scheme should ensure that most of your money is safe if the Society goes out of business.

The Association of Friendly Societies (see address on page 164) will send you a free list of its members on request.

BUYING SHARES

Because the value of shares in individual companies is so unpredictable, most people put their money into a fund which has shares in a wide range of companies. The theory is that as some fall, others will do well, leaving the fund value rising. These funds are usually sold through a structure called a 'unit trust' (see pages 103–104). The investor normally buys a number of 'units' in this fund and will get a return depending on the overall growth of the money in the fund. Some funds pay out these gains as income, while others just let it accumulate and you have to sell units to realise money from your investment.

Most funds are what is called 'actively managed' by a team of people who study the market and move the money around trying to find the best returns. The alternative is a 'passive' fund. These simply buy shares in all the companies that are in a particular stock market index, such as the FTSE 100 for example (see page 95). Because their value should follow or 'track' the value of the index they are sometimes called 'tracker' funds. One big advantage is that because tracking takes far less work than managing, their costs are a lot lower. (There is more on tracker funds on page 101.)

Picking a fund

The first thing to decide is whether you want to put your money into shares at all. After that you must choose between active or passive. Do you want your fund actively managed by a team of experts? Or do you want to hitch your money to the overall performance of the stock market?

Managed funds on average do not do very well – on average the money in them grows more slowly than the whole market or the companies in the FTSE 100. But some do better than the market – they 'outperform' it in the jargon. Adverts for these funds typically tell you how well they have done in the past. However, the Financial Services Authority is concerned that these adverts are misleading and intends to regulate the way that information is given. It has also produced research which shows that past performance is generally not a good predictor of future performance. It found that funds which had performed badly did tend to continue to be bad. But strong performing funds did not tend to show 'persistency' of that performance over a number of years. So choosing a fund on the basis of how it has done in the past is certainly no guarantee of success in the future.

The main thing that determines how well a fund does is the overall performance of the stock market and the prevailing economic conditions. It also depends on the costs and charges which are eating away at your money, on the skill of the fund manager and, to an extent not usually admitted, their luck.

So it is very hard to pick a fund that will perform well in the future and if you do so, it is largely a matter of chance. You can rely on your own judgement, or that of a financial adviser you trust, but there is no magic formula.

Despite the concerns of the Financial Services Authority and the evidence about performance, many people do want to know how the fund they are considering has performed over the last few years. This is factual information published in the monthly magazine *Money Management*, which is available from newsagents. The FSA publishes its own tables which exclude past performance – because it does not believe it is useful to know. But they do include useful information about charges and terms and where funds can be bought. They are available from www.fsa.gov.uk/consumer/compare/index.html

The other consideration about managed funds is where they are invested. There is a bewildering choice, with around 2,000 trusts available. You can invest in a particular part of the world (UK, Europe, United States of America, Asia, Japan); in a particular kind of company (emerging markets, small companies, technology stocks); and vaguer things like 'special opportunities', which basically means cheap shares that the fund manager thinks might just come right in the next year. Remember that terms like 'extra income' and 'high yield' are hopes not promises and you cannot sue if they do not happen.

Trackers

Trackers came to prominence when the value of shares seemed to rise inexorably and the average growth in the value of most managed funds was less than the growth in the indices. Putting your money in the 'index' – in the FTSE 100 for example – seemed, and for a time was, a safe bet. But after three years of falling indices that faith is not so strong – after all trackers follow the index down as well as up. However, the evidence is that trackers will probably do as well or better than managed funds with your money in the long term even when the market is falling.

In a perfect world the value of a tracker should follow the index it uses precisely. So if the FTSE 100 grows by 5 per cent, your money in a FTSE 100 tracker should also grow by 5 per cent. However, three things stop them following the fund precisely:

- Some do not buy all the shares; they buy a representative selection of them. One reason is that it can be very expensive to buy one or two shares in small companies when a new investor puts money into the fund.
- When the companies in the index change, they do not get rid of the old shares and buy the new ones at once.
- There are charges involved in buying and selling shares and there will also be an annual management charge. These charges are partly offset by reinvesting the dividend income which accrues from the shares to the fund.

So funds which track the same index can in fact show different performance. Because following the index is a matter of technical efficiency, the rule about past performance not being a guide to the future does not generally apply to trackers. If a fund follows the index accurately it means it has the procedures in place to do that simple job. A fund which does better than the index is as worrying as one which does worse – it means it is following the fund approximately and has had some luck.

Other considerations

Ethical funds: A growing number of ethical unit trusts are available which invest their money according to moral principles as well as purely investment ones. For example, you can choose to avoid such things as tobacco, alcohol, animal experiments, weapons, or pornography. Or you can positively choose to support companies with good environmental policies. You can find out more from the Ethical Investment Research Service at the address on page 166.

Non-share investments: Many funds do not put all their money in the stock market. Some make use of other investments such as bonds or even cash. These 'cash funds' can be useful when the stock market is doing badly – or rather when you expect it to continue to do badly.

Returns: Finally, you should decide if you want a regular income or if you are happy for the dividends paid to be reinvested. You can then take money out of the fund by selling units. The income is normally called a 'distribution' and may be made monthly, quarterly, twice yearly or yearly. A capital growth trust can also be called an 'accumulation' trust; the distributions are used to buy extra units to add to your holding. Some trusts try to have it both ways and are called 'balanced' – in other words they aim for some growth and some income.

Charges

Whatever fund you choose charges will be an issue, eroding the growth in the value of your money. We all hope the value of our investments will rise. But three powerful forces pull it back:

- Initial fees – many investments will charge you a fee at the start (usually a percentage of the money you invest). It may be called an initial charge or an entry fee but its purpose is the same – to take some of your money away before it is invested. It can be up to 5 per cent, although charges are being forced down, and in some cases it can be zero.

- Spread – this is the difference between the buying price and the selling price (sometimes called the 'bid' and 'offer' price). When you buy something you expect to pay more than you would get if you sell it – the turn or mark-up or profit is of course at the heart of business. But it does mean that if you buy an investment at £100 but you could only sell it at £90, you have lost 10 per cent immediately. The spread on units in a unit trusts is normally between 5 per cent and 7 per cent.
- Annual charge – most investments will charge you an annual fee to 'manage' your fund or investment. This charge can be levied even if there is little or no managing to do. Even if the 'management' results in your losing money, the charge will still be applied. Nowadays, the pressure is on funds to charge no more than a 1 per cent management fee, but higher charges are still found. Some, though, are lower.

To overcome these three powerful forces dragging your money down, it really has to grow a lot over a long period to offer you a real rate of return. Through the 1990s, the stock market was growing so strongly that these charges could easily be taken and still leave an apparently healthy growth in the investment. But as the 21st century began the market fell – by 50 per cent over the first three years – and the charges began to seem excessive.

Managed funds tend to have much higher charges than tracker funds. Managing the money requires a big research department and some very highly paid fund managers. Tracking the index is a more administrative job requiring fewer and less well paid people. So costs are lower. The charges are only one consideration, but a very big one, in deciding where to invest your money.

Unit trusts

A unit trust is the best known example of what is called a 'collective investment'. It is a fund which invests in the stock market and when you buy a share of that fund your money is spread across all the investments in the unit trust. Your share is represented by a number of 'units' in the trust.

There are two ways to buy unit trusts – either with a lump sum (usually of £500 or more) or with regular savings starting at around £25 a month.

Unit prices of the funds are published daily in newspapers and weekly or monthly in the financial magazines. Two prices are given: the lower or 'bid' price is the one at which you sell back the units to the company; the higher or 'offer' price is the one at which you buy them.

You should only buy unit trusts from a firm that is regulated by the Financial Services Authority. You can get big discounts by buying from a financial supermarket (also known as discount brokers). These can most easily be found through the Internet – a list of them is at www.find.co.uk/advice/ADB/ They are registered as IFAs to sell you financial products but they do not give advice. You agree that you will deal with them on what is called an 'execution only' basis. As a result, charges are low and any commission they earn for selling you the product is paid back (they call it 'rebated') to you. They are a very cheap way of investing if you are confident in what you want to buy.

More information about unit trusts is available from the Investment Management Association – see address on page 168.

Investment trusts

One alternative to investing through a unit trust is to buy a share in an investment trust. These are actually companies which invest in the shares of other companies. The investor buys a share in the investment trust. The value of these shares depends on two things:

- the value of the underlying assets of the company – ie the shares they have bought in other companies; and
- supply and demand for the shares on the market.

Investment trusts are freer to take risks than unit trusts and can even borrow money. As a result, the value of the shares is more likely to go up and down. There are more than 300 investment trust companies to choose from, and you can invest as little as

£25 a month. At the moment, investment trusts are not regulated by the FSA.

The Association of Investment Trust Companies (AITC) provides free factsheets and a free basic introduction called *Its for investment trusts* – see page 164 for the address.

Split-capital investment trusts

This variation on an investment trust can be very dangerous. A split-capital trust separates the capital into two or more 'classes'. Typically, shares in one class get all the income and have a fixed redemption price; they suit basic-rate taxpayers who need an increase in income, perhaps to supplement a pension. Capital shares get nothing until the predetermined redemption date when the trust is wound up and the capital appreciation of the total fund is distributed. Capital shares suit investors prepared to forgo immediate income for greater capital gain in the future. They are often called zero dividend preference shares – also known as zeroes.

Some split-capital trusts, especially those with zero dividend preference shares, ran their businesses in very risky ways, magnifying share price movements rather than reducing them. Some borrowed money from the bank to invest in more shares. Some invested heavily in other investment trusts. Both practices are legal but dangerous. The funds were marketed as low risk when they were anything but, and some ordinary investors, tempted in by promises of high returns, have lost a lot of money. Of over £8 billion invested, around £6.5 billion has disappeared. They are not regulated by the FSA. Avoid them.

Open Ended Investment Companies (OEICs)

Unit trusts and investment trusts may be replaced eventually by Open Ended Investment Companies (OEICs). An OEIC is a company which invests in shares, and investors in the OEIC buy a share in the company. They are simpler and cheaper than the other two forms of collective investment and are a common form of investment outside the UK. Like unit trusts they are 'open-ended'; in other words there is no limit to the total amount of money you can invest. Like investment trusts they are companies with boards of directors. So your investment is represented by 'shares' not 'units'. Unlike investment trusts they are regulated by the FSA.

Shares in an OEIC carry a single price at which they are bought and sold, so there is no expensive spread between the price you pay and the price you can sell at. The share price of an OEIC will move up and down each day in line with the stock market: an OEIC is, like any other share investment, for the long term.

For more information on OEICs contact the Investment Management Association at the address on page 168.

Picking shares yourself

Some people decide to do without a fund manager and to pick shares themselves and buy and sell them directly. This is a much higher risk activity and requires you to keep an eye on your investment all the time. Marconi, Cable and Wireless and Railtrack all showed us how shares in apparently solid companies can suddenly lose their value.

There is always a risk involved when putting money in the stock market, so it is usually best to get professional advice. But if you want to make your own investments – or simply want a better understanding of your broker's advice – here are some simple investment rules:

- Read the financial press and follow the radio and television programmes (see 'Publications and programmes' on pages 171–172).
- Diversification reduces risk. You may want to spread your money among fixed-interest stocks, unit and investment trusts investing in the UK and overseas markets, and UK companies with a long record of growth.

- If you want a flutter – and if you really can afford the possible loss – invest in a speculative share or two.
- Avoid investing in too many individual companies, because of the monitoring and paperwork required.

One method of safeguarding your capital – to a limited extent – is the 'stop loss' technique. You decide the maximum loss you can afford – for example 20 per cent of the price of the share. If the share price falls by this amount, you sell. If the share price goes up, your stop loss point rises with it. You can adopt a lower stop loss point of 10 per cent, for example, but this might mean that you miss out on a good rise in the price of your share.

Brokers

You cannot buy shares directly – you have to go through a broker. This is not the difficult and expensive process it used to be. Many brokers also offer an 'execution only' service – they buy and sell for you but do not give advice. The cost has fallen considerably in recent times, particularly for smaller telephone, internet or postal deals. You can find it costs only £10 to buy or sell and prices of under £20 are common. There are lots of other cheap deals around for small investments, particularly from the major banks and building societies. In addition to the broker's fee, a Stamp Duty is payable on all share purchases. The duty is 0.5 per cent of the price of the share.

When choosing a broker find out whether they will allow you to make regular monthly investments, instead of investing one lump sum. The advantage of regular investments is that they average out the price you pay for shares, so timing your purchases is not such an issue.

You can get a free list of London Stock Exchange members operating in your region from its website at www.londonstockexchange.com – click on 'membership and trading services', then 'list of members'. The Association of Private Client Investment Managers and Stockbrokers also publishes a directory of members – telephone 020 7247 7080 for a free copy or look on the website at www.apcims.co.uk

Long-term investment

Putting your money in the stock market is a long-term decision. There is no point in putting it there for a year or two. Anything less than ten years is too little. Share prices in early 2003 fell back to where they were in 1995; in other words more than seven years investment produced no growth at all. So shares are for the long term. There are three reasons for this:

- You have to recover the charges levied at the start and the effect of the spread; it takes a few years' growth to do that.
- As we have seen, stock markets do go down as well as up. Although they have always risen in the long term, we can never be sure how long the 'long term' is. There have been two 25-year periods in the last century when the value of shares was the same at the end as the beginning.
- The dividends on the shares are normally reinvested and compound interest will boost the growth over a longer period.

So if you do invest money in the stock market, make sure that it is money you do not want or need for a number of years (ten at the least and preferably more). So stock market investments should be confined to pension savings and other long-term needs. But remember that, however long you invest for, it is possible you will not get back what you have put in.

Unit-linked or with profits?

When you buy into a unit trust you can see each day the value of your units. Similarly, if you hold individual shares you can see the value of them. Investments of this sort are simple and straightforward. But they do carry the risk of what is called 'volatility' – in other words their value goes up and down all the time. And when you need to cash in your money they may be down.

Insurance companies found a way to avoid this many years ago. They invented another sort of investment which they called 'with profits'. You give them your money and they invest it, both in shares and in fixed-interest investments as they see fit. Nowadays around half or less will be in shares. The growth in the fund is paid to you in two ways:

- At the end of the year they dole out some of the profits the fund had made. This is called an annual bonus and once it has been given to you it is guaranteed (it is a bit like adding your interest onto your savings account at the end of the year). However, you never know how this bonus is worked out. In good years you will get less than the fund has grown. In bad years you will get more. That is to smooth out the ups and downs of the stock market. Most with-profits funds have paid out bonuses for the last three years even though the stock market has fallen. In other words, you are being paid money that has been held back from good years in the past.

- At the end of the investment, which might be after a set number of years or when you reach pension age, you will get a further payment called a 'final' or 'terminal' bonus. This money will be worked out by actuaries as your share of the growth of the fund while your money has been invested in it, on top of the annual bonuses you have had. This amount is not guaranteed and most insurers will not even give you an estimate of what it will be.

With-profits investments have been criticised recently for their lack of 'transparency'; ie they are hard to understand and, even when you do, you cannot work out how the 'bonuses' (which are simply the return on your investment) have been worked out. The other problem is that investors have come to expect a positive return even when markets fall for two or three years. That cannot go on forever.

TAX-FREE INVESTMENTS

Individual Savings Accounts (ISAs)

Since April 1999 there has been one way to invest money tax-free – it is called an ISA and it replaced PEPs for new investments from that date. Anyone with a PEP taken out before 6 April 1999 can still keep it (see page 111).

An ISA is not an investment itself. It is simply a way of holding an investment so that the interest, dividends and growth are free of all UK tax. The maximum amount you can invest through an ISA is £7,000 a year. All of that can be in a shares based ISA if you want, unless you have already put any money into a cash ISA (see pages 83–84), in which case you are limited to £3,000 in shares. The name Individual Savings Account is misleading for a shares ISA. It is an investment, not a savings account, with all the risks that investments carry.

There are no restrictions on the types of shares and unit trusts in which the 'equities' element of an ISA may be invested. The money does not have to be in shares. It can be in corporate bonds or gilts or other fixed interest investments. There is no fixed term to an ISA – you can invest and can take your money out whenever you wish. The only restriction is that you can only put in either £3,000 or £7,000 during the year. Although ISAs are billed as 'tax-free', it is worth considering what that means in practice. First, the 10 per cent basic-rate tax on the dividends paid on the shares can be reclaimed by the fund. However, this will only be allowed until April 2004. Higher-rate taxpayers do not need to pay that on the dividends. The interest earned on other investments is free of tax and saves the 20 per cent basic-rate tax and higher-rate tax if you pay it. Second, there is no Capital Gains Tax on the growth in the fund.

So the main advantage of the tax-free status of ISAs is to people who pay higher-rate tax or who have capital gains in excess of the annual £7,900 limit. For most ordinary investors the tax-free status of shares ISAs is limited and will virtually disappear in 2004. However, the tax advantages still apply to ISAs invested in corporate bonds and gilts where income will be free of tax.

There are other advantages to ISAs. The Government has set certain standards for ISAs. They are called the 'CAT standards' and cover charges, accessibility, and terms; ie the level of charges, the degree of accessibility, and the terms on which the different elements are offered. The CAT standards do not offer guarantees on the performance of your investments within the ISA. But if you go for a CAT standard ISA you know that the costs will be low and the terms good.

Most unit trusts and other investments in funds can be bought through an ISA and that is the normal way you will be offered them. Some ISAs specialise in fixed-interest products like corporate bonds or gilts or a mixture of the two.

Personal Equity Plans (PEPs)

Tax-free shares investment before 6 April 1999 were called Personal Equity Plans or PEPs. Anyone holding a PEP at 5 April 1999 is allowed to continue to hold it indefinitely, but not add to it. You can, however, switch your investment from one PEP to another. The tax relief and tax advantages of PEPs are the same as for ISAs.

ANNUITIES

One way of providing yourself with a definite income for the rest of your life is by purchasing an annuity. You give a lump sum to an insurance company and it gives you a guaranteed income for life. When you die, the income dies with you and if there is anything left of the lump sum, the insurance company keeps it. You can protect yourself against dying early and losing a lot of money for your heirs by taking a 'guaranteed annuity' which will carry on paying for a minimum period even if you die shortly after taking it out – typically they last for five years from when you buy them.

These 'purchased life annuities' should be distinguished from the annuity you have to buy with a pension fund. Although they are the same in principle, they are treated differently for tax purposes. With a pension fund annuity, the whole of the income is treated as taxable income. That is done because all contributions into a pension are free of tax, so the Treasury takes its tax when the income is generated. A purchased life annuity is counted in a different way. Part of the money you get each month is treated simply as a return of your capital and is not taxed. Only the extra money – in effect the interest your money is earning – is counted as income and is taxed. The Inland Revenue decides how much is taxed depending on your age and sex; the older you are, the more of your money is tax-free.

If you buy an annuity you must make several decisions:

- Flat or rising – a flat annuity will be fixed for life and so after 20 years of inflation will be worth far less than at the start. A rising annuity will keep up with inflation, or will rise at 3 per cent or 5 per cent each year. Of course, it will start off far lower.
- Guaranteed or not – do you want the annuity to pay out for a guaranteed period even if you die meanwhile?
- One life or two – if you are married or live with a partner, you can ensure that the annuity continues to be paid to

them if you die first. This choice will of course significantly reduce the income from your annuity.

- Impaired life – if you are a smoker or have a disease which could shorten your life, then you will get a higher income from an annuity.
- Market-related – although annuities used to be paid as a definite sum each month, some of them are now related to a fund which is invested. As a result these annuities can go up and down as the fund does better or worse. However, you can pick a unit trust which is invested in safe, fixed interest investments if you wish.

The minimum sum required to buy an annuity is around £5,000. The income may be paid in arrears or in advance, half yearly, monthly or annually. How much you get from each £1,000 of capital depends on your age, the insurance company chosen, the conditions of the annuity and interest rates at the time of purchase. The amount you get as income from each £1,000 – called the annuity rate – has fallen by almost half over the last 15 years. That is partly because interest rates have fallen, and partly because people are living longer. The difference between the best and worst annuity is considerable, so shop around carefully. Once you have bought it you are stuck with that decision for life.

An annuity which pays an income for a short fixed term can be useful to bridge a gap before an improvement in your circumstances. If, for example, you are made redundant at 60 but your pension is paid from the age of 65, your redundancy payment could provide an annuity income in the meantime. However, before investing in an annuity, you should get independent advice and consider other investment possibilities.

MORE COMPLICATED INVESTMENTS

There is one golden rule of investment – if something seems too good to be true it probably is. There are many tempting offers in financial services which promise guarantees of high returns at little risk. They are generally best avoided. You cannot defy gravity and returns on capital at the moment are low. But then, so is inflation. If you are not greedy and are sensible you should be able to make reasonable returns at low risk.

CREATING AN INVESTMENT PORTFOLIO

'An investment portfolio' may sound a bit grand but all it means is that you have thought about your money and you have followed the basic rule – diversify. It is much safer not to have all your eggs in one basket. Most of the grief investors experience is because they put all or a substantial part of their money in one place – and it failed. Apart from spreading the risk, you are unlikely to find a single savings or investment product that meets all your financial needs. Some money should be instantly available for emergencies, some you may want to tie up for a period to produce a fixed income, whilst other money may be savings for a particular expense. You must also assess what financial advisers call your 'risk profile' which is a fancy way of saying – are you willing to risk losing money for the chance of making more than the boring 3 to 4 per cent you can get through safe investment?

The way some of them talk about it, you would think that the risk was one way – that you always made money by taking a risk. Of course you do not. Risk means risk – you could lose some or, in extreme cases, all of your money. Investment is like that: you are trusting other people with your money, and their incompetence, greed, or dishonesty will cost you dear.

So when you are asked to take a risk, recognise that investment performance is not a one-way bet. Of course, there is some protection against dishonesty with the various compensation schemes. So it is vital to make sure that your adviser, and the funds they are putting your money in, are regulated with the Financial Services Authority. But incompetence is not covered by any protection scheme – if someone calls a scheme 'high growth' and after two years your money has halved in value that will not normally be covered by any protection from the authorities or the courts.

It is also important to make sure that even your day-to-day money and your emergency fund is working hard in an account that pays interest. So make use of your tax-free cash ISA. Put some money in guaranteed fixed interest investments to bring you an income. If, for the long term, you do want to risk some money on the stock market, make sure you diversify with money tied to different parts of the economy, perhaps even different parts of the world – and watch those charges as they will eat away at your investment every single year whatever it makes or loses.

You may also want to put money into the stock market month by month rather than all at once. That way if the market falls you have not put all your money in when it is high, and if it rises then the money you put in earlier seems good value. The technical term for it is 'pound cost averaging'. Of course, in a market that is only falling that simply ensures you lose your money more slowly.

If you want a financial adviser to help you with all this, it is a good idea to put in writing what you want and what risk, if any, you are willing to take. Generally the more risk you take, the higher the adviser's commission.

Setting up your own portfolio

Instead of using a financial adviser, you can set up your own portfolio. If you do not have £10,000 or more, then it is probably the best thing to do anyway. The first step is to be clear about your objectives: is your main need for income or capital growth? Do you need to make sure that your capital is safe?

Even if you want complete safety you can save a lot of money by rearranging your savings and investments. A useful rule of thumb is to keep an emergency fund equal to about three months' income in an easy-access account that does not penalise you for withdrawals. Always remember to check interest rates before you invest. They may have changed, and nowadays changes are usually down. Keep an eye on them too. Many products start off well and get worse over time. New often is best when it comes to interest rates. Read the conditions attached to any financial product before you buy and make sure they are suitable for you. There can be penalties for taking your money out of an investment early – even safe ones like National Savings and Investments or guaranteed income bonds. Look carefully at investments which promise high rates of return to make sure that your capital is not at risk. Finally, check the status of the organisation that will be investing your money for you. If it is registered in the UK it will normally have better protection when things go wrong.

Tax considerations

Tax considerations should not drive your investment or savings decisions, but making full use of your tax allowances can save you a lot of money. The earlier part of the book gives illustrations of how tax can be saved. Couples who are still receiving the Married Couple's Allowance may want to consider transferring part or all of it from the lower (or non) taxpayer to the higher taxpayer.

A couple may also be able to save tax by transferring any investments where the income is taxable to the spouse with a lower income – for example if one spouse pays tax at the basic rate while the other is a non-taxpayer.

Tax-saving tip: If you have a joint account and one account holder pays no tax, they can recover the tax paid on half the interest the account earns. Most banks will agree to pay half the interest gross. Ask for form R85.

If you are increasing your income through your investments, be aware of the impact this can have on your age-related Personal Allowance (see pages 15–16). Most financial advisers will not be aware that people over 65 can pay an effective rate of tax of 30 per cent or 33 per cent with an income of around £18,000 a year.

The portfolios

In the following pages we look at six sample portfolios. They were constructed with interest rates and investment rules that were current at the time of writing, using information from *MoneyFacts* and other sources. Although every effort has been made to be accurate, they may not include all charges and the products mentioned may not be available in the future. Readers must always check current rates and conditions before making decisions and moving their money.

The portfolios are for sums of £13,000 to £36,000. Some of the investors are married and some are single; some are working and some retired. The youngest is 55 years old and the oldest is 70. They all have fairly modest amounts of money, yet the improvements to their finances can be dramatic through a combination of maximising the interest earned, minimising the tax they pay, and looking at their investment objectives and needs. Generally they have taken little risk and almost all the extra income or savings are guaranteed.

These six portfolios are purely for general illustration, and must not be taken as firm recommendations for anyone whose circumstances may appear to match the examples. Readers should always consider fully their own individual needs before saving or investing, and take professional advice where appropriate.

Summary of investors

Investor	Age	Non-investment income £	Total amount to invest £	Investment aims
1 Ron Single employed	55	£17,500	£13,800	Higher income, some capital growth, reducing tax
2 Jane and John Retired	65	£15,340	£14,500	Increased income, no risk, reducing tax

3 May Single employed	55	£24,000	£16,200	Capital growth, higher pension, reducing tax
4 Nooreen Widow	70	£4,641	£24,000	Income and safety money, reducing tax
5 Ed and Meg Ed works, Meg doesn't	60	£31,000	£26,000	Capital growth, reducing tax
6 Mary and Sean Just retired	65	£24,500	£36,000	Income, reducing tax

I RON

Ron is 55 years old and earns £17,500 a year. He belongs to his company pension scheme. He has to make mortgage payments of £400 a month, but these end when he is 60. He has £10,000 savings which are have been in an Abbey National Investor 60 account for some years. That pays him just 2.03 per cent and the interest is paid quarterly. His salary is paid into his Barclays current account, which he has had for years, but earns only a nominal 0.1 per cent interest on the current balance. Ron also has a TESSA which has just matured. He paid it into his current account and spent the interest it had earned on a new sofa. But he has the £3,000 balance still there to reinvest which he can put into a cash ISA if he does so within six months. He has no other investments or assets apart from his house. He is happy to rely on his pension when he retires at 60, but wants to earn a bit more interest and pay less tax. He does not need the income from his savings to come quarterly. He would rather save it up until he retires.

Ron's portfolio

Ron's first step is to move all his money out of the Abbey National account. Unfortunately he has to wait 60 days or pay penalties. So he writes to Abbey National giving 60 days notice and waits for his cheque. Meanwhile he has to reinvest his maturing TESSA within six months of its maturing. He puts it into a West Bromwich Building Society TESSA-only ISA. That pays 4.35 per cent fixed and guaranteed for five years. Although he might get a shade more elsewhere it would not be a fixed rate. He is happy to have it tied up until he retires. When his money arrives from Abbey National he puts £3,000 into a mini-cash ISA to earn interest tax-free. He chooses Kent Reliance Building Society which is paying 4.4 per cent with instant access, by post, if he wants it.

For the rest he decides to try out an internet account and chooses Northern Rock Tracker Online which pays 4 per cent. He puts £4,000 in there to see how it works out, but he wants to keep the remaining £3,000 in a branch-based account. He decides on reflection to leave it with Abbey National in its Direct Saver account as he knows where the branch is and it does pay 3.1 per cent – a lot better than he got on his old account with them. He then chooses a current account and Halifax seems best. There is a branch in the town near him and he is happy with 3 per cent interest. Ron is never overdrawn but he gets a £100 interest-free overdraft in case something does go wrong.

Ron

	Invested	Interest rate	Amount received	After tax	Notes
Original portfolio					
Current account	£800	0.10%	£0.80	£0.64	Barclays current account
Matured TESSA	£3,000	0.10%	£3.00	£2.40	ditto
Savings account	£10,000	2.03%	£203.00	£162.40	Abbey National Investor 60
Total	£13,800		£206.80	£165.44	Ron pays tax on all his interest

Revised portfolio

Current account	£800	3.00%	£24.00	£19.20	Halifax
TESSA-only ISA	£3,000	4.35%	£130.50	£130.50	West Bromwich fixed for 5 years
Cash ISA	£3,000	4.40%	£132.00	£132.00	Kent Reliance Building Society
Online account	£4,000	4.00%	£160.00	£128.00	Northern Rock Tracker Online
Branch savings account	£3,000	3.10%	£93.00	£74.40	Abbey National Direct Saver
Total	**£13,800**		**£539.50**	**£484.10**	Ron saves £318.66 a year – £6.13 a week.

Commentary

Altogether Ron has more than doubled the income his savings bring in, gaining £318 a year. Next April he can move another £3,000 into a mini-cash ISA if he wants, and he can move his existing £3,000 as well if he finds a better rate somewhere else. He has a number of different accounts and if the internet account does work out he may want to shift more money there to maximise his interest and give up the branch-based savings account altogether.

2 JANE AND JOHN

Jane and John are both retired. Jane stopped her part-time job last year when John retired at 65. Embarking on retirement they want to maximise their income. John has a company pension of £8,500 a year which will rise roughly with inflation. They both have a State Pension – John has £83.50, which includes a bit of SERPS, and Jane has £48.10, based on John's contributions plus a small amount of graduated retirement benefit from her work in the 1960s. Their mortgage is paid off.

Their only asset other than their home is £12,000, which is made up mainly of John's pension lump sum together with a bit of savings. It is in a building society account in John's name with Alliance & Leicester but despite the 30 day notice to get the money out, it only earns 1.65 per cent gross. They also have about £2,500 in a current account as they like to know they can write a cheque out for any sudden expense or treat. They are not greatly concerned about capital growth but want their £12,000 to boost their pensions which come to just under £15,000. They do not want to take a risk with it. They want access to some of it but think they can afford to tie up around half of it, maybe a bit more, for a few years.

Jane and John's portfolio

Jane and John look at options for increasing their income. The first thing to do is to consider moving their current account. They never go overdrawn and have a reasonable balance and all their pensions are paid direct into it. The balance varies but averages £2,500 over the year. They do not have a computer so an internet account is out of the question. They decide to move their current account to Alliance & Leicester. It pays good interest and if you have the current account you can get a very good rate on savings too. The current account pays 3.1 per cent and they will earn just over £60 a year. However, as it is a joint account, and Jane pays no tax, they can register on form R85 to have half the interest paid without tax being deducted and that adds another few pounds.

The next step is to find a mini cash ISA for £3,000 of savings. They want instant access and the local Cheltenham and Gloucester is just down the road so they take that at 4.25 per cent. They then put another £3,000 into the Alliance &

Leicester PhoneSaver Premier account in Jane's name so no tax is paid on that. It pays 4.15 per cent which they get in full as they register to have interest paid gross. That leaves £6,000 to invest for a bit longer.

They decide on a Pensioners Bond Series 31 from National Savings & Investments. It pays 3.6 per cent over five years. Interest is paid monthly and gross. It is taxable but they decide to put it in Jane's name so no tax is due on it – they are aware that means the money is Jane's and not 'theirs'. The Pensioners Bond ties the money up for five years but they know what it will bring in and that is a great help.

Jane and John

	Invested	Interest rate	Amount received	After tax	Notes
Original portfolio					
Current account	£2,500	0.10%	£2.50	£2.00	HSBC current account
Savings account	£12,000	1.65%	£198.00	£158.40	Alliance & Leicester 30-day notice
Total	£14,500		£200.50	£160.40	
Revised portfolio					
Current account	£2,500	3.10%	£77.50	£69.75	Alliance & Leicester Premier current account
Cash ISA	£3,000	4.25%	£127.50	£127.50	Cheltenham and Gloucester
Telephone savings account (Jane)	£3,000	4.15%	£124.50	£124.50	Alliance & Leicester PhoneSaver Premier

Pensioner Bond series 24 (Jane)	£6,000	3.60%	£216.00	£216.00	National Savings Pensioners Guaranteed Income Bond Series 31
Total	£14,500		£545.50	£537.75	Jane and John save £377.35 a year or £7.26 a week.

Commentary

They have gained £377 a year (more than £7 a week). Their extra cash comes from two sources. First, they choose higher interest rate products. Second, they avoid paying almost any tax by using tax-free savings and making use of Jane's tax-free allowance – she can have £6,610 a year of income before tax is due. That option is of course only available to couples in this position. They like National Savings & Investments products because they are backed by the Government and so are completely safe. There is no risk, other than that they have taken out a fixed interest rate product from National Savings & Investments and of course they should keep that money untouched for five years to take full advantage of it. The portfolio also allows plenty of cash, including their current account, for holidays, gifts or other spending, but all their money is earning something.

3 MAY

May is a 55-year-old single woman who earns £24,000 a year. She keeps about £1,200 on average in her current account. She has savings of £10,000 in a building society postal account paying 1.25 per cent gross and £5,000 in a bank which pays 2.25 per cent but offers a cash card and instant access. May now wants to use her £15,000 to provide her with more money when she retires, which she does not expect to do until she is 65. She is prepared to lose some current investment income to provide capital growth.

May's portfolio

May is getting a reasonable income from her two accounts, but if she wants capital growth with safety she will have to put at least part of her money elsewhere. The first step is to move her current account so that her day to day money earns something. Her standard Lloyds TSB account pays 0.1 per cent. May is a computer buff and she is happy to do all her banking online in future. So she moves her current account to cahoot which pays her 3.74 per cent on the balance. It is the best current account rate especially as she does not want a chequebook – she pays everything online. She also moves another £5,000 leaving her with an average of £6,200 in that account earning interest and available at once if she needs it.

She puts another £3,000 into a cash ISA and again she wants instant access, so she goes for the Kent Reliance as it offers the best rate at the moment at 4.4 per cent. That is tax-free and next April she can move another £3,000 from her cahoot account to the cash ISA. May is already more than £250 better off, and she still has £7,000 she can invest for capital growth. She is happy to tie it up for 10 years until her anticipated retirement but wants to be able to get it out after five years 'just in case'.

May should check her company pension scheme. It may be that her employer will match any extra contributions she pays in. If so, she should pay more into that. If not, she should pay into a stakeholder pension. If she pays in £2,808 out of her savings the Chancellor will add £792, making £3,600 invested. That pension fund will be invested on the stock market and, as she is already over 50, will be available to her at any age she chooses. A quarter of it can be taken as a lump sum, but the rest will have to be used to buy an annuity so it is as well to leave it in until she is at least 65. She chooses a stakeholder fund that has low charges, 0.75 per cent a year, and tracks the FTSE 100 stock-market index. All share investments are a gamble but she thinks that is the safest one there is and, like many people, she believes that after three years of falling the stock market is likely to rise.

May

	Invested	Interest rate	Amount received	After tax	Notes
Original portfolio					
Current account	£1,200	0.10%	£1.20	£0.96	Lloyds TSB
Postal savings account	£10,000	1.25%	£125.00	£100.00	Leeds & Holbeck Capital 7
Instant access account	£5,000	2.25%	£112.50	£90.00	Halifax instant saver
Total	£16,200		£238.70	£190.96	
Revised portfolio					
Current account	£10,392	3.74%	£388.66	£310.93	cahoot – no cheques
Cash ISA	£3,000	4.40%	£132.00	£132.00	Kent Reliance
Total income				£442.93	May is £251.97 a year better off – £4.85 a week.
Stakeholder	£2,808.00		£972.00	£972.00	Tax relief + 5%
Total	£16,200				And she has gained tax relief into her pension fund.

Commentary

May decides to stop there, leaving the balance of her money in the cahoot account earning reasonable interest while she decides what else to do. She is more than £250 a year better off through investing her cash and current account more sensibly and tax-free. She has also invested some money for her pension in the future. Next year she can decide to put another £3,000 into her cash ISA and another £2,808, if she wants, into her stakeholder pension.

May has a useful mixture of cash which is safe, and of money in a stakeholder which is on the stock market. That money is at risk, but if the market grows, her money will grow with it and over 10 years she is confident that it is a good place for it. Of course, the market may fall. But as the Chancellor has added 28 per cent to it, the chance of it falling below the total she invested herself is remote although of course it may happen. If her fund grows by 5 per cent a year after charges, then she will have gained £972 in year one from tax relief and growth. At that rate, the fund will be worth nearly £4,600 after five years and more than £5,800 after ten years for an outlay of £2,808.

4 NOOREEN

Nooreen is a widow of 70 with one daughter and two grandchildren. She has £24,000 which she and her late husband Navtej saved up. But she has to spend some of it to make ends meet and has never really taken much notice of it or the income it earns. She is just glad when she gets a bit added to her account once a year. She still has £7,000 languishing in a Cheltenham and Gloucester Gold account earning 0.5 per cent. She has a pass book and draws out some of it as and when she needs it. The rest is in a slightly better LloydsTSB Instant Gold Savings account earning 1.05 per cent. Her State Pension is £89.25 a week, which includes her late husband's SERPS. She draws it in cash each week from the post office and does not have a current account as she manages her money in cash. But she knows that she will have to have a current account soon when order books are phased out. She cannot claim Minimum Income Guarantee because her savings are well above the £12,000 maximum. However, she will be able to claim Pension Credit in October. She pays no tax as her income is well below her tax allowance.

Then Nooreen starts to think about her savings and how hard she and Navtej worked for them. She thinks that a higher income for the same amount of savings would give her the opportunity to use the extra money in different ways: perhaps a few extra gifts for her grandchildren.

Nooreen's portfolio

Nooreen's main objective is to increase her income. Her money is in bad accounts and she could earn more almost anywhere. She should also register to have her income paid gross, without tax deducted.

She is a very cautious woman and does not want to lose any of her capital. She does not use a computer and likes to be able to go into a branch of her bank or building society. Out of her £24,000 she decides to keep £3,500 in a local bank. She opts for a Woolwich Card Saver account that gives her 2.72 per cent with the interest paid monthly. She uses her card but can withdraw over the counter if she pays a £1 fee. She registers to have any interest paid to her gross.

For the rest she decides to put £20,000 in Birmingham Midshires fixed term bonds. She chooses a mixture – half over one year earning 4.07 per cent and half over three years earning 4.46 per cent. Both pay the income monthly. That allows her to think about her money again in a year and see how she is managing and how much of her £3,500 is left in the Woolwich. Interest is paid monthly and she registers to have it paid gross as she pays no Income Tax.

Nooreen

	Invested	Interest rate	Amount received	After tax	Notes
Original portfolio					
Current account	£7,000	0.50%	£35.00	£28.00	Cheltenham & Gloucester Gold
Savings account	£17,000	1.05%	£178.50	£142.80	LloydsTSB Instant Gold Savings
Total	£24,000		£213.50	£170.80	She pays tax on all her interest
Revised portfolio					
Current account	£3,500	2.72%	£95.20	£95.20	Woolwich Card Saver – monthly interest
One year bond	£10,000	4.07%	£407.00	£407.00	Birmingham Midshires 1 year
Three year bond	£10,000	4.46%	£446.00	£446.00	Birmingham Midshires 3 year
Total	£23,500		£948.20	£948.20	Boosts her monthly income by £64.78. She is £777.40 a year better off.

Commentary

Nooreen has thought about her savings for the first time since Navtej died and realises how much it has cost her to do nothing about them before. She has increased her income by £777 a year and she now gets a regular £71 a month credited to her Woolwich account which she can take out with her card as she wants it. She has stopped paying any tax. Of course, she also has to run down her money in Woolwich a bit during the year but that has been allowed for in the income projections. She can review her finances again next year and in three years. She has taken no risks except that the three year income may not look so good if interest rates rise a lot in those three years.

5 ED AND MEG

Ed and Meg have been married for 32 years and are both 60 years old. They have to pay nearly £400 a month on their mortgage, which ends in five years time. It is an endowment mortgage but if the endowment does not cover the whole loan, Ed will have a lump sum from his company pension to do so. Ed earns £31,000 a year. Meg has spent most of her life looking after the family, all of whom have now left home. Her outside jobs have been low paid and non-pensionable. However, she did work from the age of 16 until she was married at 28. Since the children left home she has had a few part-time jobs but not paid full National Insurance contributions. They have £25,000 in a building society instant access joint account and £1,000 in their current account.

Ed and Meg's portfolio

Meg paid full National Insurance contributions for more than ten years when she was young. She gets a pension forecast from the Department for Work and Pensions on form BR 19 and finds that she has earned a small pension of £23.55 a week, which includes some graduated retirement benefit she paid for in work in the early 70s. As her 60th birthday was eight months ago, she claims it at once. She is disappointed that it is backdated for only three months – but when the money arrives she is pleased to have more than £250 plus a small regular income of her own. When Ed reaches 65 she will get a higher pension on his contributions which will be paid instead of her own pension. But at least she has it for nearly five years.

Ed, meanwhile, checks up on his company pension scheme. Ed finds that the rules have changed since he last looked and he can put some more in and his employer will match it. He gets full tax relief on his contributions so he opts to put in another £50 a month which costs him £39 because he gets full tax relief. His employer matches it, so for an outlay of £39 he gets £100 into his pension fund.

Now they look at their mortgage. Although it has only five years to go they are paying 5.84 per cent interest on the full loan of £40,000, which costs them £195 a month. They investigate remortgaging and discover that they can reduce that to 4.45 per cent, saving them £45 a month. There are fees of £450 to pay and letters to write but it is worth it. Once those have been paid the savings cover the extra contributions into Ed's pension.

Ed now turns to their current account. He has already moved his current account once but it took ages and was not really any better. But now that the banks are committed to moving standing orders and direct debits quickly and easily, he decides to move it again. He opts for a smile account, even though it is not the highest interest rate, because he and Meg like the Co-operative Bank's ethical policies. He is happy to go online with his finances. That earns him 3 per cent and he and Meg usually have about £1,000 in there, so it seems worthwhile. They register on form R85 to have half the interest paid gross as Meg is a non-taxpayer. Next step is a mini-cash ISA and again they stick with smile (not the best rate around but they like the Co-op). Ed puts the maximum £3,000 in his name and at 4 per cent gets £120 a year tax free.

Now they want to invest the rest and they know that Meg is a non-taxpayer – she can have £4,615 a year before tax is due and her income at the moment is barely £1,200. So they decide that the rest will be in her name.

Ed wants to make the money grow – they don't need income from it but he does want more cash when he retires. He reckons £3,000 in a cash ISA is enough; the rest he wants to grow as much as possible. In discussion with Meg they decide to split it – half on the stock market and half in a safe growth product. The latter is the National Savings Capital Bond Series 10 which guarantees 3.9 per cent growth per year. They invest £11,000 and after five years they will get back £13,319. The interest is paid gross and the money is invested in Meg's name so they do not have to pay any tax on it. Ed insists that the other £11,000 goes in the stock market. Even though the price of shares has fallen over the last three years, he is still confident that historically shares do better than other investments. He wants some of his money to be there when the present doldrums blow away. He does a lot of research but eventually decides to go for low charges and a tracker fund that follows the FTSE all share index. No-one knows how well it will do. Ed puts a modest 5 per cent a year in the growth rate and hopes for more. They use the same tracker fund but put £3,000 in the fund in Ed's name as a mini-shares ISA and the rest in Meg's name so there is no risk of tax being paid.

Ed and Meg

	Invested	Interest rate	Amount received	After tax	Notes
Original portfolio					
Current account	£1,000	0.10%	£1.00	£0.80	Halifax
Savings account	£25,000	3.35%	£837.50	£670.00	Cheltenham & Gloucester branch 10
Total	£26,000		£838.50	£670.80	
Revised portfolio					
Current account	£1,000	3.00%	£30.00	£24.00	smile
Cash ISA	£3,000	4.00%	£120.00	£120.00	smile
Fixed interest bond	£11,000	3.90%	£429.00	£429.00	National Savings Capital Bond Series 10 – paid on maturity

Extra pension for Meg			£1,224.60	£1,224.60	
Total guaranteed			£1,803.60	£1,797.60	
Tracker ISA	£11,000	5.00%	£550.00	£550.00	Not guaranteed
Total	£26,000		£2,353.60	£2,347.60	

Commentary

Ed and Meg have looked at all their finances. They have saved money on their mortgage and put that straight into Ed's pension fund, gaining tax relief and doubling it at once by the generous benefits from his employer. Meg has gained more than £1,200 a year by claiming her own pension – many married women do not realise they are entitled to one.

They have also saved tax and boosted income. Moving some money to a riskier investment has left them nearly £100 a year worse off in guaranteed returns on their investments, but if Ed's hopes materialise on his tracker fund, then they will do a lot better, making nearly £500 a year more on their investments.

In five years' time, when retirement looms, they will be free to look again at their safe, fixed interest investment, and they will be able to see if Ed's stock market gamble has paid off.

6 MARY AND SEAN

Mary and Sean are both 65 years old and have just retired with company pensions of £10,000 and £6,000 respectively, as well as full State Pensions. Mary wisely never paid the married woman's stamp. So their income is around £24,500 a year. Their endowment has matured and the mortgage has already been paid so it is all profit. They both took a lump sum from their pension. Together with their savings they have £35,000 to invest and no children to leave it to.

They are at the age when they want extra income for holidays and leisure rather than capital growth. Their current account is with

Nationwide where they earn 2.5 per cent on their £1,000 credit balance, and they temporarily deposit the £35,000 in a Nationwide Cashbuilder account they have had for some years. It earns 1.65 per cent and Sean wonders why it pays less than the current account. But he leaves it while they decide what to do.

Mary and Sean's portfolio

They consider an annuity, but the rate for two people at 65, with a guarantee of ten years for the last survivor, does not produce the income they want and all the money is lost – it is a once and for all decision which they do not feel ready to make.

As they love computers they go for a cahoot current account which will pay them 3.64 per cent with a chequebook. They tend to keep around £1,000 in their current account so they open it up with that much. Next, they are both taxpayers so they both immediately open a mini-cash ISA with the maximum £3,000. They go for Cheltenham and Gloucester at 4.25 per cent.

They have plenty of capital and want to spend some of it in a methodical way. So they buy a gilt. They choose Treasury 2008 9 per cent stock. They have to pay around £125 for each £100 of stock, but that means they get a return of 7.2 per cent on their investment. The downside is that when they redeem it in 2008, they will only be given back £12,000 for their £15,000 of stock. In other words they have spent £3,000 of it over that period. But they don't mind. The *Financial Times* tables show it is a real return over the period of 4 per cent which they are happy with. The income is paid in April and October and will help with holidays. The tax does not have to be paid on it until 31 January when they fill in their self-assessment forms.

That leaves them £14,000. They decide the best thing to do with that is to put it in cash ISAs each year as the £3,000 allowance comes available. Meanwhile they put it away for a year in a fixed interest bond from Birmingham Midshires. You need at least £10,000 but it pays 4.07 per cent, which is taxable. They can review it in a year, putting another £6,000 between them in cash ISAs and then think what to do with the balance.

Mary and Sean

	Invested	Interest rate	Amount received	After tax	Notes
Original portfolio					
Current account	£1,000	2.50%	£25.00	£20.00	Nationwide Flex
Savings account	£35,000	1.65%	£577.50	£462.00	Nationwide Cashbuilder
Total	£36,000		£602.50	£482.00	
Revised portfolio					
Current account	£1,000	3.64%	£36.40	£29.12	cahoot cheque
Cash ISA (Mary)	£3,000	4.25%	£127.50	£127.50	Cheltenham & Gloucester
Cash ISA (Sean)	£3,000	4.25%	£127.50	£127.50	Cheltenham & Gloucester
Fixed rate bond 1 year	£14,000	4.07%	£569.80	£455.84	Birmingham Midshires
Gilt Treas 9% 08	£15,000	7.20%	£1,080.00	£864.00	April and October
Total	£36,000		£1,941.20	£1,603.96	An extra £1,121.96 a year (£21.58 a week)

Commentary

The aim of this portfolio is to increase the amount of spending money. This has been achieved through maximising tax-free income, tying up money for a period, swapping some capital for cash now through the gilt, and making their current account earn money as well. They are more than £1,100 a year better off, although some of that is the return of capital on their gilt.

Next April they can look at putting more into an ISA and perhaps a bit into something more risky. In six years their gilt matures and they can look at it again and may decide they are then old enough to realise some of the value of their home through an equity release scheme, or they could consider taking out an annuity.

Improving your Finances

The previous section was about saving and investment in its traditional form – making the most of money you already have. This section explains how you can boost your income in other ways.

For people who have not yet retired, it looks at last-minute strategies for topping up your pension. There is also information on using your home to raise capital and income, on insurance policies for older people, on the financial planning implications of debt and redundancy, and on making a Will and funeral planning.

PENSION PLANNING

If you are within a few years of retirement, it may not be too late to do something about boosting your pension. In fact, as a result of the new tax rules, even if you have already left work you may still be able to add to your pension. The first thing you should do, however, is find out how much pension you are currently on target to receive.

State Pension

The youngest age to qualify for the State Pension is 65 for men and 60 for women. You can get a bigger pension if you defer drawing it to a later age. The State Pension age for women will be raised for women retiring on or after 6 April 2010 and will be 65 for all those retiring in 2020.

If you have worked and paid full National Insurance contributions for most of your working life, you will get the full basic State Pension. This year it is £77.45 a week (for a single person). If you have not paid full National Insurance (NI) contributions for all your working life, the Basic Pension may be reduced. The lower contributions paid by some married women do not count towards the Basic State Pension.

Whatever your Basic Pension, it may be boosted by graduated retirement benefit (Graduated Pension) earned between 1961 and 1975. You may also get Additional Pension, also called SERPS, on your NI contributions paid from April 1978 to 2002. Since April 2002, contributions earn State Second Pension (S2P) rather than SERPS. Both SERPS and S2P are earnings-related state pensions. Some people who paid into a company pension, or since 1988 a personal pension, may have been 'contracted out' of SERPS or S2P and not earned any extra pension for those years.

A widow or divorcée under 60 can be credited with her late or ex-husband's NI contributions in order to fill in gaps in her own contribution record. This useful rule is applied automatically – no application is needed. However, it does mean that widows or divorcées should be careful when considering remarriage. If you marry again before you reach 60, you lose the right to be credited in this way and will have to rely on your own contributions, or those of your new husband once he reaches 65 and retires. So it may be worth delaying the wedding until you reach 60. If you have already started drawing a State Pension in your own right, it does not alter on remarriage.

If you are under pension age and want to know how much your State Pension will be, you can get a form for an estimate from the Pension Service by phoning 0845 3000 168 (8am–8pm, Monday to Friday). Or you can go online at www.thepensionservice.gov.uk/atoz/atozdetailed/rpforecast.asp

---

You can find out more about the State Pension from the Age Concern book *Your Rights* (see page 174).

Private pensions

As well as the benefits from the State, there are different types of private pensions that you may have paid into and which you can start drawing when you retire. They are:

- occupational pensions – a pension scheme run by an employer; and
- personal pensions – which you have contributed to yourself. The new stakeholder pensions are a kind of personal pension.

Each of these comes in several different types.

Pension from your job

There are two main sorts of occupational pension:

- Final salary schemes, which guarantee the pension you get as a certain percentage of your salary in the last years of employment. Typically you would get 1.25 per cent of your final year's salary for each year in the scheme. So after 40 years' work you would get a pension of half the amount of your pay in the final year before you retire. Some will offer a cash lump sum as well. Altogether benefits cannot exceed two thirds of your final pay. Such schemes are mainly found in the public sector or from some bigger companies. In some schemes, especially in the public sector, the pension is increased each year in line with the rise in prices. In others it is not. With some schemes, your pension will be reduced by the amount of your State Pension when you draw it. These pension schemes can also be called 'defined benefit' schemes because it is the amount of the pension which is guaranteed, not the contributions you pay.

- Money purchase schemes, which store up all the contributions made into your pension throughout your life into your own pension 'pot'. When you retire you have to use that money saved and the interest it has earned to buy a pension for yourself. The amount you get will depend on long-term interest rates as well as your age at the time you retire – the older you are the more you will get – and your sex. Women get less than men for the same pension fund because they live longer. These pension schemes can also be called 'defined contribution' schemes because it is the amount you pay in which is fixed, not the pension you get at the end.

At the moment, the most you can pay into your company scheme is 15 per cent of your gross pay, although that will change in the next couple of years. Most company schemes take far less than that and you can make up the difference by paying into Additional Voluntary Contributions (AVCs). AVCs are designed to top up your company pension. These contributions are paid into a separate money purchase scheme either through your employer or, if you choose, separately from your employer, in which case they are called Free-standing Additional Voluntary Contributions (FSAVCs). Since April 2001, if you earn £30,000 or less, you can also pay up to £2,808 into a stakeholder pension on top of any occupational pension you may have, and the Chancellor will top this up by £792 to make a gross contribution to your pension fund of £3,600.

Money-making tip: Check for old pensions you have forgotten about with the Pension Schemes Registry (address on page 169). It has details of 200,000 pension schemes and can tell you how to make contact with any past scheme.

If your employer did not have an occupational pension scheme which you can join and is not contributing towards a group personal pension for you, then, in most cases, since 8 October 2001 that employer has to offer you 'access' to a stakeholder pension scheme and offer to deduct and pass on contributions for you.

The big advantage of most occupational pension schemes is that your employer also contributes to your fund. So if your employer has a scheme to which they contribute it is always worth joining. If you do not, you are volunteering for a pay cut. However, many employers who now offer access to a stakeholder scheme do not contribute to it. So the scheme they recommend may not be the best one for you.

Personal pensions

Any pension scheme not related directly to your employer is called a personal pension. They come in three sorts depending when you started contributing to them:

- Before July 1988 – retirement annuity contracts or Section 226 pensions
- From 1 July 1988 – personal pension plans
- From 6 April 2001 – stakeholder pensions – a special sort of personal pension.

When stakeholder pensions were introduced the rules about contributing were relaxed and now apply to personal pensions as well. The rules for retirement annuity contracts are slightly different.

All contributions to a personal pension are now paid net of basic-rate tax relief. In the past you paid in £100 out of your income before tax and payments into a retirement annuity contract are still paid in this way. But with personal pensions you now pay in £78 and the Chancellor pays in the other £22. If you are a higher-rate taxpayer you can then recover £18 tax when you fill in your self-assessment form. So your net contribution for £100 in your pension is just £60.

If you are working and you are not paying into an occupational pension scheme, or if you are self-employed, the amount that can be paid into a personal pension depends on your age. The percentages are of your gross pay (or £99,000 if that is lower) and include the amount paid in by the Chancellor. If you are still paying into a retirement annuity contract the limits are lower but there is no earnings ceiling. These contribution limits will be scrapped and replaced by a simpler rule, probably from April 2004.

Contribution limits to a personal or stakeholder pension

Age	Contributions	
	Personal/ Stakeholder	Retirement annuity contract (begun pre-June 1988)
61 and over	40%	27½%
56 to 60	35%	22½%
51 to 55	30%	20%
46 to 50	25%	17½%
36 to 45	20%	17½%
under 36	17½%	17½%

If you have not paid in the full amount allowed in any tax year, you can make a payment up until the following 31 January and have it counted as if you paid it in during the previous tax year. So if you were short of the maximum in 2002–2003 you can pay in extra contributions before 31 January 2004 and they will count in the 2002–2003 tax year.

If you work and pay into an occupational pension scheme you can still pay into a stakeholder pension as long as you earned less than £30,000 in this tax year or last. A stakeholder pension will almost always be a better alternative to AVCs as the charges are likely to be lower and, unlike AVCs, you can take up to 25 per cent of your pension fund in cash, tax-free from the age of 50. You are limited to a gross contribution of £3,600 a year into the stakeholder pension. That means you pay in £2,808 and the Chancellor pays in another £792.

Apart from tax relief there are a couple of other savings that paying into a pension can help with:

- If you are a parent with a child going to university, a pension contribution reduces your 'residual income' and lowers the contribution to the student loan you would otherwise have to make. You could then pass this on to your children.
- Occupational or personal pensions can be 'contracted out' of the State Second Pension (or previously SERPS). That means you pay lower National Insurance contributions and more money goes into your occupational or personal pension.

You can also pay into a stakeholder pension at any age up to 75 even if you are not in work. That means that parents or grandparents can start one for a child. Remember, however, that no money can be taken out of the pension until that child is 50 years old. The annual contribution limit is the same – you cannot pay in more than £2,808 and the Chancellor pays in the tax relief, making a maximum of £3,600 altogether.

Before the law allows a scheme to be described as 'stakeholder' it must be registered with the Occupational Pensions Regulatory Authority (Opra), and meet certain conditions. The two important ones are:

- The only charges allowed are a deduction of up to 1 per cent of the fund each year. (Other personal pension arrangements can have an array of complex charges, although the competition from stakeholder pensions means that many personal pensions have lower and simpler charges than they used to.)

- You must be allowed to stop and start payment, increase or decrease the amount, and transfer the money elsewhere, without paying extra charges.

Because the charges are so low, there is little room for advisers to earn money from them. So if you want detailed advice – as opposed to straightforward information – about whether a stakeholder pension is right for you, or which one to choose, you may have to pay more. If you already contribute to a personal pension – or its predecessor a Section 226 retirement annuity contract – find out whether it will benefit you to carry on paying in, or start instead with a stakeholder pension. It will depend on how the charges are structured; some personal pensions penalise you for making any changes at all, while others are more flexible. You can pay into a stakeholder scheme as well as a personal pension scheme at the same time, so long as you do not go above the limits set out in the table above.

Part-time workers

Part-timers – or people who used to work part-time – who have been excluded from a firm's pension scheme may have additional rights as a result of European law. Part-timers must now be allowed to join a pension scheme on equal terms to full-timers. People who were excluded from schemes in the past may be able to claim backdated pension rights for years as far back as 1976. However, you must have made the claim before leaving that job, or within six months afterwards. Ask your union or the Pensions Advisory Service (OPAS) for assistance (see page 170).

Approaching retirement

All personal pensions (including stakeholder schemes) and a growing number of company schemes save money up for you while you pay in but, when you retire, you have to convert the fund into an income. Your pension will depend crucially on the size of that pension fund. So it is important as you approach retirement to reduce the risk that is taken with your money. Typically, your fund should slowly be moved out of stock market investments and into safer places – the industry likes to call them 'less volatile investments' – like bonds and gilts, or even cash, to consolidate past investment gains. Some will automatically switch you out of high-risk investments during the last few years before retirement. This is called a 'lifestyle' arrangement. If your policy does not have an automatic switching facility, ask the adviser who sold you the policy for advice on how and when to switch. But beware of 'churning' – moving your investments around in order to generate commission for the adviser.

When to retire

Most company pension schemes have a normal retirement age of between 60 and 65, but you may be able to start drawing some pension from the age of 50. Personal pensions, including stakeholder, allow you to take the benefits from any age between 50 and 75 (60 and 75 for retirement annuity contracts).

Although early retirement can seem attractive, it will reduce significantly the pension you get. In a company final salary scheme you will have fewer years' service so you will get a smaller proportion of your salary. If you are in a money purchase scheme or a personal pension then retiring early will cost you dear. Your fund will be smaller as it will have been building up for less time. And the annuity you buy with it will give you a lower income because you will be drawing your pension for longer. You will need a very big pension fund indeed to be able to retire at 50. In future it is likely that people will have to retire later, not earlier.

Once you do decide to take the benefits from your pension you are very constrained in what you can do with it. Normally you have to buy an annuity. You give an insurance company your fund, and it promises to pay you a pension for the rest of your life. That is called an annuity. The insurance company uses its knowledge of life expectancy and investments to work out how much it can give you year by year and still make a profit at the end.

When do I have to buy an annuity?

Once you reach 75 you have to use most of your pension fund to buy an annuity – although you can normally take a quarter of it as a tax-free lump sum. Before that age you can choose to keep your fund intact and take some income out of it. That is called 'income drawdown' but the amount you can take is limited to roughly what a good annuity would pay and the company selling you the drawdown scheme will charge fees. For people with less than around £250,000 in their fund, drawdown is not a good idea. You may as well buy an annuity. Of course, if interest rates rise in the future, it would pay to wait to buy an annuity. But if they fall, waiting could cost you dear.

So what choices do I have?

The most important choice is the freedom to go to any insurance company to buy your annuity. It is called your 'open market option'. Using that choice can mean a much higher income every year for the rest of your life. The difference can be startling. Even among the top ten providers the difference between the best and the worst income can easily be £1,000 a year. Choosing the right annuity provider can boost your income by up to 30 per cent for life. The company that runs your pension fund is usually *not* the best company to buy your annuity from. So get advice and choose the best.

What other choices do I have?

You must also choose whether to take a fixed income which stays the same every year, or whether you want your income increased each year in line with inflation. Although inflation is low now, over the last 20 years prices have risen on average by 3.9 per cent a year. If you had an annual income of £10,000 20 years ago, you would need £21,595 a year to be as well off now. Most people do not choose an annuity that rises with inflation because it starts a lot lower. For example, a man aged 65 with £100,000 pension fund could buy an annuity of around £7,250 from the best provider. But if he wanted an income that rose each year with inflation, he could only get £5,600. Of course, the £7,250 would never change. The £5,600 would go up each year in line with inflation. But it is a tough choice when you have just retired and need more money.

Cash

Not all your fund has to be converted into an annuity. You can keep some of your fund as a tax-free cash lump sum. Normally this is 25 per cent of your fund but you cannot keep any of the money you have put into AVCs – all that has to be put into an annuity. Keeping cash gives you a lot of flexibility. You can invest the money yourself and perhaps use it to buy a different sort of annuity which could boost the income you get – or, of course, you can spend some of it to give yourself a retirement treat.

Pension problems

Over the past few years, the Financial Services Authority has been investigating claims that people selling personal pensions persuaded millions of employees to leave perfectly good occupational pension schemes and take out inferior personal pensions. It is now too late to make a claim for compensation for this mis-selling scandal, and if you had already registered a claim, it should have been cleared up by June 2002. A separate investigation is going on into the mis-selling of Freestanding AVCs. If you feel you were encouraged to buy these products with false promises, then you may be able to get compensation if you make a complaint.

Every occupational pension scheme must have an internal disputes procedure, and financial services companies must also have complaints procedures. The Pensions Advisory Service (OPAS) will be able to give information and advice where the pension scheme administrator cannot help you, or help you put in a complaint and follow it through (see page 170 for the address). If OPAS cannot resolve the problem, you can take your case to the Financial Ombudsman Service.

Employers' pension funds are owned and controlled by independent trustees and should be safe if the company goes bust. However, there is no guarantee that the assets of the pension fund will be sufficient to pay the pensions that the employer has promised. Existing pensioners get priority and whatever is left is used to buy pensions for those who have not yet retired. The fund should have enough in it to meet certain minimum standards – that is called the 'Minimum Funding Requirement' or MFR. However, even this minimal protection is expected to be changed soon. Meanwhile, the costs and risks of providing final salary schemes are leading many companies to close them to new members, and a few have also closed them to existing members as well, moving everyone to the inferior money purchase schemes. Existing members will get the rights they have already earned, but when they retire the pension they get is likely to be far less than they were expecting.

Your Guide to Pensions, published annually by Age Concern Books, gives information about the various types of pension that are available (see page 174).

LIFE INSURANCE

Life insurance is a simple product – you pay money and if you die then your heirs get a lump sum. But over the years that simple product has been confused with investment to the extent that the simple life insurance product is often now called 'protection'. Before paying into a life insurance policy, you should think about your dependants, if you have any, and how much money they will need if you die. Many people have too much life insurance – it is easy to sell and pays well for the person who sells it. If you are a member of an occupational pension scheme, some life cover is likely to be included while you are still at work. If you have a mortgage, you may have taken out insurance to pay off the loan in the event of your death.

Life insurance can be divided into four types:

- whole life
- term or temporary insurance
- endowment
- annuity.

A whole life policy pays out on death whenever that occurs. Because we all die, it will eventually pay out and is in effect an investment product as much as a life insurance product. It is often unnecessary and expensive. For anybody over 50, it should be considered only when there is a potentially serious Inheritance Tax liability, and all other steps to minimise that liability have been taken. Even then, term assurance is more appropriate.

Term insurance is basic and cheap; the cost will rise the older you are when you take out cover. You pay premiums for a limited period, but the policy pays out only if you die within the period. It is useful while you have dependent children. Once the youngest reaches a certain age, the insurance will stop. The latest variant being offered by the insurance world is a scheme which provides compensation in the event of certain serious illnesses. However, for anyone over 65 this 'dread disease' cover is likely to be very expensive and probably inappropriate.

Endowment insurance is a method of saving for a guaranteed payment at the end of a fixed number of years, or earlier if you die before then. Unlike term insurance, money always comes back – either to you or, if you die within the period of the insurance, to your heirs. Endowment assurance policies were often sold alongside mortgages. Usually such a deal was a mistake. Endowment assurance is relatively expensive and once the need for the lump sum goes, people may be tempted to surrender the policy. However, it is unlikely to be a good idea – especially if you are getting tax relief, which is available only on those started before 14 March 1984. If you can afford to, it is usually best to keep paying into the policy until its end. If you must get rid of it, you will always be better off selling it through a specialist endowment trader. Get professional financial advice on the options, particularly the tax implications. The firms that specialise in the purchase and sale of endowment policies belong to a trade association: the Association of Policy Market Makers (see page 165).

YOUR HOME

For most people their home is their most valuable asset. Whether you are just approaching retirement or already retired, you may well find that there are several things you can do to make it work for you.

Moving house

Many people see retirement as the signal to sell the family home and move somewhere smaller. That can reduce your outgoings and may also produce a useful lump sum which could then be invested for capital growth or to boost retirement income.

However, many people have found their dream cottage by the sea turn into a nightmare of isolation from family and friends. Nor should you underestimate the cost of moving house. With agent's fees and removal costs (and Stamp Duty for property over £60,000 – see page 60), it could be as much as 10 per cent of the value of your new home.

Paying off your mortgage

There is little point in investing money at 3 per cent or 4 per cent before tax and paying 5 per cent or 6 per cent on your mortgage loan. Simple arithmetic says the best return on your money is to pay off the debt. Of course, if you have other debts, your mortgage is almost certainly the least expensive of them, so pay off other debts first. But once you have done that, if you get a lump sum – perhaps from your pension, from a maturing endowment, or inheritance – consider paying off your mortgage. On the other hand, if you can afford your mortgage payments, you may feel happier to have some money in the bank for emergencies. It is all a matter of personal preference.

One alternative to paying your mortgage off is to change your lender. You can often get a very good deal by moving your mortgage, which will save you money in the short term. Of course, the older you are the harder it is to remortgage. Before going ahead with any changes in your mortgage situation, always check costs against gains. Get advice from a qualified mortgage broker (they will not be regulated by the Financial Services Authority until October 2004 but make sure the lender is authorised by the FSA). Some mortgage brokers charge you a fee and earn commission from the lender. Others do not charge you a fee.

Letting your home

One way to raise money from your home is to let it. Income from a lodger who shares your home is tax-free up to £4,250 a year. In order to qualify, the lodger has to live in your home, not a self-contained part of the building where you live. The rent is free of Income Tax. If you receive a self-assessment form, the amount of rent does not have to be declared, but you do need to say that you have received it and are claiming Rent a Room relief. Inland Revenue leaflet IR 87 *Letting and your home* has more information.

Some people rent their home out as a film or TV set. It is very lucrative but can be devastatingly disruptive. Don't worry if your home is small; many TV dramas are set in very modest houses. Check in *Yellow Pages* under 'TV, Film and Video Production' for agencies. Or you can contact the BBC which welcomes details of properties. Just call 020 8225 9133 for a questionnaire about your home. If you live in a city you may be able to rent out parking space.

Raising money from the value of your home

You may be able to use the capital value of your home to raise cash – while continuing to live in it – by taking out a home reversion scheme, a roll-up loan plan or a home income plan. In general the older you are, the higher the income or capital you will receive from these schemes.

Nowadays, the best way to release some of the value of your home is often through a home reversion scheme. With this, you give a proportion of the value of your property to a reversion company which gives you a lump sum, or in some cases a guaranteed income, in exchange. You continue to live in the house under a lifetime tenancy agreement. On your death, or on the death of both partners in the case of a married couple, the proportion of the property sold passes to the reversion company. Some schemes have special features, such as index-linking the annuity income to the value of all properties in the scheme. If you start by selling a proportion of your property, you can often sell a further proportion later and so top up your income or capital later and you also share in the rising value of property. You can move in some circumstances and you are protected if you have to go into a care home.

An alternative is a lifetime mortgage (which used to be called a roll-up loan). You borrow money using your home as security, like a mortgage. The interest is not paid back but 'rolled-up', increasing the size of the loan each year. When you die or move into a care home, your home is sold and the total debt is paid, leaving you, or your heirs, the balance. In the past these schemes were not recommended as the debt could soon exceed the value of the property, but modern schemes guarantee that will not happen. Nevertheless, you should take care before embarking on one.

Traditional home income plans are now almost extinct. They worked by lending you money against the value of your home which you then used to buy an annuity giving you a guaranteed income for life. Part of that was used to pay off the loan interest, leaving the rest for you to spend as you wish. At the end of your life, the home is sold to pay off the debt. The schemes became a lot less attractive when tax relief on mortgage interest was abolished in the March 1999 Budget. Although existing plans retained this advantage, it was not available for schemes taken out after that date.

The problem with all these schemes is that you give up a large amount of the value of your home but get relatively little money in return. Always think very carefully and take advice from a professional adviser who specialises in them before taking out one of these schemes.

Age Concern Books annual publication *Using Your Home As Capital* (see page 174) gives more detailed information about home reversion schemes and the other ways of raising money from your home. Age Concern Factsheet 12 *Raising income or capital from your home* lists companies that market schemes – see page 171 for details of how to obtain Age Concern factsheets.

GENERAL INSURANCE COVER

Once you reach 50 you can find much better deals on insurance for your home, your car, and even travel.

Money-saving tip: If you have not changed your insurer since you hit 50, shop around for a cheaper deal. Buying insurance over the Internet can also save you money.

Of course, it can be a different matter once you are 70 or 75 – you may find that the same companies that were keen to have your business suddenly do not want to know. If you are 70 or over, many motor insurance policies will have certain restrictions, and you may be required to have a medical examination each year when the contract is due for renewal.

Travel insurance can also be difficult as you get older. Travel insurance policies carry certain restrictions, depending on your age, which can void certain sections of the policy. This is particularly relevant to medical insurance, and you should check your policy wording carefully or discuss it with the company concerned before you travel. Age Concern Insurance Services* has a special policy for older travellers. Always look around before taking out travel insurance to make sure that you are being offered a competitive rate.

Money-saving tip: If your buildings insurance is bought through your mortgage lender, it will almost certainly be cheaper to get it through another insurer.

Insurance to provide private health care is generally very expensive for older people. It is probably better to save some money in cash knowing that it is there in case you need to pay for relief from a painful condition before the National Health Service will provide it.

There is too much uncertainty about insurance for long-term care for it to be worth buying at the moment.

Age Concern benefits financially from the sale of all insurance products provided by Age Concern Insurance Services

DEBT

Almost every adult is in debt at some time – through borrowing money to buy a cooker, a fridge, a TV, a car, or indeed a mortgage to buy a home. Credit cards are a useful means of managing short-term debt. Buying something costing hundreds or thousands of pounds would not be possible for most people if they could not spread the cost over months or years. Credit has never been easier, total debt has never been larger and of course some people do get into difficulties. Often it is for unforeseeable reasons – redundancy, bereavement, relationship breakdown, or the sudden onset of illness. But, of course, some people do allow their debts to become unmanageable through their own actions – or inactions. Whatever the cause, few things are so devastating mentally and physically as serious money worries – and fears about the poverty, homelessness or even bankruptcy which may follow. So it is very important to take action and sort out debt before it goes too far. Remember:

- Some debts have more serious consequences than others. So draw up a list of debts that must be paid because of the penalties.
- Companies you owe money to would rather be spoken to than ignored. Tell them the problem; do not throw letters in the bin unanswered.
- They would also rather be paid something than nothing.
- There is help available.

You do not have to deal with debt alone. Money advice centres operate in many towns and cities. National Debtline, run by the Birmingham Settlement (address on page 165), has a telephone helpline for those with money problems. The Consumer Credit Counselling Service (CCCS) on Freephone 0800 138 1111 also offers debt counselling. The local Citizens Advice Bureau (CAB) can also help – you can find the address in the phone book or ask at your local library. The Bankruptcy Advisory Service offers help and advice to those facing bankruptcy (see page 165 for the address).

It may be possible to get a grant from a charity. *The Guide to Grants for Individuals in Need* lists such grant-giving charities. It is published by the Directory of Social Change and should be available through your local library or Citizens Advice Bureau.

Managing Debt from Age Concern Books provides detailed information for people facing financial problems – see page 175.

REDUNDANCY

Losing your job late in life is a frightening thing. If you hear you are going to be made redundant, take time to recover from the shock before you make any plans. Make sure that your employer writes to you setting down the terms of your departure and confirming that it is due to redundancy. Without that you may find problems with the Inland Revenue and the Department for Work and Pensions over tax or claiming benefits.

Redundancy pay

When you leave you will get all the wages that are owed to you, including any amounts owing for holiday pay or pay in lieu of notice. You should also get redundancy pay. If your contract of employment specifies an amount of redundancy pay – for example one month's pay for each year's service – then you should get that. You might also receive an ex gratia payment, perhaps for particular services you have rendered. Redundancy pay up to £30,000 is tax-free, but holiday pay and pay in lieu of notice are taxed as normal.

Even if there is no entitlement to redundancy pay in your contract, your employer has to pay the statutory minimum amount. You are entitled to redundancy pay if you have been working for your employer, full or part-time, for two years or more, and you are at least 20 and below 65 years old – or below the normal retirement age at your place of work if that is less than 65. The amount of pay is related to your age, your years of service and your weekly wage up to a maximum of £260 a week from February 2003. By law you are entitled to a written statement of how your redundancy pay has been worked out.

Age at redundancy	Pay entitlement for each year's service with that employer
41–64	One and a half weeks
22–40	One week
18–21	Half a week

An employee who is within 12 months of their 65th birthday will get their statutory redundancy pay reduced by one-twelfth for each complete month after their 64th birthday. This 'tapering' reduces entitlement to nothing by the time the employee reaches the age of 65.

If your employer goes out of business the Government will pay you the statutory minimum redundancy pay. You can get help and advice from the Redundancy Payments Office (see page 170 for the address).

Jobseeker's Allowance

If you are unemployed, looking for work, and under pension age (65 for a man, 60 for a woman) you should be able to claim a benefit called Jobseeker's Allowance (JSA). It comes in two sorts. Contribution-based JSA is paid for up to six months on the basis of your National Insurance contributions. There is also an income-based JSA which may top up the contribution-based JSA or replace it entirely when it ends after six months. Both sorts of JSA are taxable. You will need to sign and keep to a Jobseeker's Agreement, which will show what steps you intend to take to find work.

Contribution-based JSA is £54.65 per week for those aged between 25 and pension age. If you have an occupational or personal pension of more than £50 per week, your JSA will be reduced by the amount that is over £50. There are no additions for dependants.

You may be able to claim income-based JSA if you are under pension age and have a low income and savings of no more than £8,000. For men aged 60–64 this limit is £12,000 up to 5 October 2003 when it will be removed. You must not work for 16 hours a week or more and your partner must not work for 24 hours a week or more.

Leaving work

When you finally leave your job and sign on for Jobseeker's Allowance, you are faced with two problems. First, you have to come to terms with the sudden change from enforced work to enforced leisure. Second, you have to decide how best to use the lump sum paid on redundancy – although of course it may not be very much.

Make haste slowly is the solution to both problems. Put the money received into the highest-interest instant access account that you can find, and then have a pause for thought. Whether you look for more work will depend on your age, temperament, commitments and income, and the state of the economy. Ideas about how best to use your lump sum can be found on other pages of this book.

FUNERAL PLANNING

Many people choose to plan ahead for their funeral and if you do it is a good idea to leave some written instructions in or with your Will about whether you wish to be buried or cremated and where you wish the ceremony to take place.

You may also want to ensure that enough money will be readily available to cover the likely cost of the funeral. If you will leave sufficient money in your estate to cover your funeral, you can let the cost be paid out of that. Some people like to save up for their funeral through a prepayment plan, such as those offered by Age Concern*, the National Association of Funeral Directors, some friendly societies and a few insurance companies. There have been cases of people putting money into this type of plan and losing it. If you do sign up to a plan of this kind, make sure that your money goes into a separate trust account with a well-known firm as the trustee. Also, check what effect the plan might have on any means-tested benefits, such as Minimum Income Guarantee or Pension Credit, that you may be able to claim.

A widow or widower who cannot afford a funeral for a deceased spouse may be able to claim a Funeral Payment from the local social security office. To get one they must be entitled to Income Support, Minimum Income Guarantee or Pension Credit, Housing Benefit, Council Tax Benefit, income-based Jobseeker's Allowance or higher rates of Working Tax Credit or Child Tax Credit. Payments are normally made to the partner of the deceased person or to the closest relative or, if there are no relatives, to a close friend. If there is sufficient money in the deceased person's estate when that is finally sorted out, then the funeral payment will have to be repaid. The money comes from the Social Fund and you can get form SF 200 and advice from the local social security office. Get this information before making the arrangements.

Age Concern Factsheet 27 is called *Arranging a funeral* – see page 171 for details of how to obtain Age Concern factsheets.

* Age Concern benefits financially from the sale of Age Concern funeral plans

MAKING A WILL

It is very important to make a Will, especially if you live or work abroad. A Will ensures that your assets are disposed of as you wish and your dependants are provided for. It can also help to ensure that your heirs do not pay tax unnecessarily.

In England and Wales, a Will must be signed and witnessed by two people who are not beneficiaries of it. In Scotland a Will written in your own handwriting – technically called a holograph – does not need to have the signature witnessed. It is also important to make sure that your Will is somewhere it can easily be found by your relatives, preferably lodged in a bank or with a solicitor.

If you die without a Will – what the law calls 'intestate' – your money and goods are divided among members of your family according to rules laid down by law; if none of these family members are alive, what you have left goes to the State. Your partner is automatically entitled to money in a joint bank account. The surviving holder of a joint post office savings account or National Savings certificates (except for those nominated before May 1981 to be paid to someone else) must notify the death of the joint holder on form DNS 904, obtainable at any post office counter.

You can draw up a simple Will by yourself, or use a Will-writing service such as that provided by Age Concern England, or, if you prefer, seek professional advice.

Age Concern Factsheet 7 *Making your Will* gives information both on writing your own Will and on seeking professional advice – see page 171 for details of how to obtain Age Concern factsheets.

Further Information

This part of Your Taxes and Savings *gives details about national organisations that might be a source of help and further information. In addition there is a list of publications and Age Concern factsheets as well as radio and television programmes covering money matters. Also included is an index to help you find the information you require in this book.*

Age Concern Funeral Plan
Freepost MID 30010
Sutton Coldfield
West Midlands B72 1BR
Tel: 0800 731 0651
The Age Concern Funeral Plan enables you to arrange and pay for funeral arrangements in advance.

Age Concern Insurance Services
New City House
PO Box 591
Preston PR1 1WX
Enquiry line: 0845 603 4529
For home insurance protection for buildings and contents. Also offers motor insurance, travel and pet insurance.

Association of British Insurers
51 Gresham Street
London EC2V 7HQ
Tel: 020 7600 3333
Website: www.abi.org.uk
Offers advice and information on a wide range of insurance products. Runs a quality standard scheme called Raising Standards which assesses financial services products – see the website www.raisingstandards.net for more information.

Association of Friendly Societies
10–13 Lovat Lane
London EC3R 8DT
Tel: 020 7397 9550
Website: www.afs.org.uk
Produces a free brochure called 'Making friends with your friendly society'.

Association of Investment Trust Companies (AITC)
Durrant House
8–13 Chiswell Street
London EC1Y 4YY

Tel: 020 7282 5555
Information Hotline: 0800 085 8520
Website: www.aitc.co.uk
For a range of factsheets explaining various aspects of investment trusts.

Association of Policy Market Makers
APMM
The Holywell Centre
1 Phipp Street
London EC2A 4PS
Tel: 020 7739 3949
Website: www.apmm.org
Specialises in the purchase and sale of second-hand endowment policies. Brochure and list of associate members sent on request.

Bankruptcy Advisory Service
2 Greenways
Swanland Hill
Hull HU14 3JN
Tel: 01482 633035
Provides help and advice for people facing serious debt or bankruptcy.

BIBA (British Insurance Brokers Association)
14 Bevis Marks
London EC3A 7NT
Tel: 020 7623 9043
Website: www.biba.org.uk
The leading UK trade association for general insurance brokers.

Birmingham Settlement
318 Summer Lane
Newtown
Birmingham B19 3RL
Tel: 0121 248 3000
National Debtline: 0808 808 4000
Website: www.birminghamsettlement.org.uk
Runs National Debtline and offers factsheets which are free to individuals in debt.

Building Societies Association
3 Savile Row
London W1S 3PB
Tel: 020 7437 0655
Website: www.bsa.org.uk
The trade association for all building societies.

Chartered Institute of Taxation
12 Upper Belgrave Street
London SW1X 8BB
Tel: 020 7235 9381
Website: tax.org.uk
Professional body for tax advisers.

Council of Mortgage Lenders
3 Savile Row
London W1S 1PB
Tel: 020 7440 2255
Website: www.cml.org.uk
Association representing mortgage lenders. Only recorded information and range of consumer information booklets available.

Debt Management Office
Eastcheap Court
11 Philpot Lane
London EC3M 8UD
Tel: 020 7862 6500
Website: www.dmo.gov.uk
Administers gilts for the Government and produces a free guide for private investors.

Ethical Investment Research Service
80–84 Bondway
London SW8 1SF
Publications orderline: 0845 606 0324
Tel: 020 7840 5700
Website: www.eiris.org
Publishes a range of publications, including a guide to choosing a financial adviser.

Financial Ombudsman Service (FOS)
South Quay Plaza
183 Marsh Wall
London E14 9SR
Tel: 0845 080 1800
Website: www.financial-ombudsman.org.uk
Helps consumers resolve complaints about most personal finance matters. The service is independent, and free to consumers.

The Financial Services Authority (FSA)
25 The North Colonnade
Canary Wharf
London E14 5HS
Switchboard: 020 7066 1000
Public Enquiries Office: 0845 606 1234
Website: www.fsa.gov.uk
Regulates most investments and financial service providers.

Financial Services Compensation Scheme (FSCS)
7th Floor Lloyds Chambers
Portsoken Street
London E1 8BN
Tel: 020 7892 7300
Website: www.fscs.org.uk
Pays compensation to customers of a financial services company which goes out of business.

IFA Promotion Ltd (IFAP)
2nd Floor 117 Farringdon Road
London EC1R 3BX
Tel: 020 7833 3131
Hotline: 0800 085 3250
Website: www.unbiased.co.uk
Phone their hotline for a list of independent financial advisers in your home or work area.

Inland Revenue Capital Taxes
For current information about Inheritance Tax:

England and Wales	Scotland	Northern Ireland
Ferrers House	Meldrum House	Level 3
PO Box 38	15 Drumsheugh	Dorchester House
Castle Meadow Rd	Gardens	52–58 Great Victoria St
Nottingham	Edinburgh	Belfast BT2 7QL
NG2 1BB	EH3 7UG	

Probate and IHT Helpline: 0845 30 20 900
Orderline: 0845 234 1000
Website: www.inlandrevenue.gov.uk

Inland Revenue Savings, Pensions, and Share Schemes Division
Yorke House
PO Box 62
Nottingham NG2 1BG
Tel: 0115 974 1600
Website: www.inlandrevenue.gov.uk
For enquiries about pensions.

Institute of Chartered Accountants in England and Wales
Chartered Accountants' Hall
PO Box 433
London EC2P 2BJ
Tel: 020 7920 8100
Website: www.icaew.co.uk
For information about choosing and using a chartered accountant.
For Scotland, ring: 0131 347 0100.

Investment Management Association
65 Kingsway
London WC2B 6TD
Tel: 020 7831 0898
Information Hotline: 020 8207 1361
Website: www.investmentfunds.org.uk
For factsheets and a list of all the available unit trusts and OEICs.

Law Society
113 Chancery Lane
London WC2A 1PL
Tel: 020 7242 1222
Website: www.lawsoc.org.uk
For complaints about solicitors.

National Association of Funeral Directors
618 Warwick Road
Solihull B91 1AA
Tel: 0121 711 1343
Website: www.nafd.org.uk
Offers code of conduct and procedure.

National Savings & Investments
Blackpool FY3 9YP
Tel: 0845 964 5000
Website: www.nsandi.com
For information about all products from National Savings and Investments.

Occupational Pensions Regulatory Authority (Opra)
Invicta House
Trafalgar Place
Brighton
East Sussex BN1 4DW
Tel: 01273 627600
Website: www.opra.gov.uk
The statutory regulator for the operation of occupational and stakeholder pension schemes in the UK.

Office of Fair Trading
2–6 Salisbury Square
London EC4Y 8JX
Enquiries: 08457 22 44 99
Leaflets: 0870 606 0321
Website: www.oft.gov.uk
Examines services to consumers.

Pension Schemes Registry
PO Box 1NN
Newcastle Upon Tyne NE99 1NN
Tel: 0191 225 6316
Website: www.opra.gov.uk/registry/regmenu.shtml
Information service for tracing pensions.

Pensions Advisory Service (OPAS)
11 Belgrave Road
London SW1V 1RB
Helpline: 0845 601 2923
Website: www.opas.org.uk
For questions and complaints about pensions.

Redundancy Payments Office
Customer Service Unit
7th Floor
83–85 Hagley House
Birmingham B16 8QG
Free helpline: 0500 84 84 89
Website: www.redundancyhelp.co.uk
For information about matters relating to redundancy.

Stock Exchange
Old Broad Street
London EC2N 1HP
Public information line: 020 7797 1372
Website: www.london stockexchange.com
For free booklets and a list of brokers for small investors.

TaxAid
Tel: 020 7803 4959
(10–12am Mondays–Thursdays)
Website: www.taxaid.org.uk
Offers free advice, on the telephone or by appointment only, to people with tax problems who cannot afford an accountant.

PUBLICATIONS AND PROGRAMMES

Age Concern Information Line/Factsheets subscription

Age Concern produces more than 45 comprehensive factsheets designed to answer many of the questions older people (or those advising them) may have. Topics covered include money and benefits, health, community care, leisure and education, and housing. For up to five free factsheets, telephone: 0800 00 99 66 (7am–7pm, seven days a week, every day of the year). Alternatively you may prefer to write to Age Concern, FREEPOST (SWB 30375), ASHBURTON, Devon TQ13 7ZZ.

For professionals working with older people, the factsheets are available on an annual subscription service, which includes updates throughout the year. For further details and costs of the subscription, please write to Age Concern at the above Freepost address.

Magazines and newspapers

Most daily newspapers provide information on personal finance. Often supplements on particular aspects of saving or borrowing appear on a particular day or at the weekend. Relevant magazines include:

Choice. For practical advice on personal finance but with wider interests for older people.

Financial Times. For Stock Exchange and other market prices, and money market funds.

Investors Chronicle. For simply written articles on companies in the news and topical articles of interest to investors.

MoneyFacts. Monthly publication giving interest rates for all financial institutions. Annual subscription £67.50, from

MoneyFacts House, 66–70 Thorpe Road, Norwich NR1 1BJ. Tel: 01603 476476.

Moneywise. Monthly magazine giving financial information in easy-to-read, lively format. Available from newsagents.

What Investment? For investment and tax planning articles.

Radio and television programmes

There are a number of programmes that may be of interest, including:

Money Box, BBC Radio 4 on Saturday and Monday afternoons.

The Money Programme, BBC TWO on Sunday evenings.

Working Lunch, BBC TWO on weekday lunchtimes.

ABOUT AGE CONCERN

This book is one of a wide range of publications produced by Age Concern England, the National Council on Ageing. Age Concern works on behalf of all older people and believes later life should be fulfilling and enjoyable. For too many this is impossible. As the leading charitable movement in the UK concerned with ageing and older people, Age Concern finds effective ways to change that situation.

Where possible, we enable older people to solve problems themselves, providing as much or as little support as they need. A network of local Age Concerns, supported by many thousands of volunteers, provides community-based services such as lunch clubs, day centres and home visiting.

Nationally, we take a lead role in campaigning, parliamentary work, policy analysis, research, specialist information and advice provision, and publishing. Innovative programmes promote healthier lifestyles and provide older people with opportunities to give the experience of a lifetime back to their communities.

Age Concern is dependent on donations, covenants and legacies.

Age Concern England
1268 London Road
London SW16 4ER
Tel: 020 8765 7200
Fax: 020 8765 7211
Website:
www.ageconcern.org.uk

Age Concern Scotland
113 Rose Street
Edinburgh EH2 3DT
Tel: 0131 220 3345
Fax: 0131 220 2779
Website:
www.ageconcernscotland.org.uk

Age Concern Cymru
4th Floor
1 Cathedral Road
Cardiff CF11 9SD
Tel: 029 2037 1566
Fax: 029 2039 9562
Website:
www.accymru.org.uk

Age Concern Northern Ireland
3 Lower Crescent
Belfast BT7 1NR
Tel: 028 9024 5729
Fax: 028 9023 5497
Website:
www.ageconcernni.org

PUBLICATIONS FROM AGE CONCERN BOOKS

Money matters

Your Rights 2003–2004: A guide to money benefits for older people
Sally West

A highly acclaimed annual guide to the State benefits available to older people. Contains current information on Income Support, Pension Credit, Housing Benefit, State Pensions, Incapacity Benefit and Jobseeker's Allowance, among other matters, and provides advice on how to claim.

£4.99   0-86242-363-5

Your Guide to Pensions 2003–2004: Planning ahead to boost retirement income
Sue Ward

An essential guide for people in their mid-life years who are keen to improve their pension arrangements. It explores, in detail, the main types of pension scheme – state, stakeholder, occupational and personal – and offers guidance on increasing their value.

£6.99   0-86242-378-3

Using Your Home as Capital 2003–2004
Cecil Hinton and David McGrath

This best-selling book for homeowners, which is updated annually, gives a detailed explanation of how to capitalise on the value of your home and obtain additional income.

£4.99   0-86242-377-5

Changing Direction: Employment options in mid-life: 2nd edition
Sue Ward

The new edition of this topical and highly practical book is designed to help those aged 40–55 get back to work. It helps readers understand their own skills, shows how to look for a job and guides readers through the many positive steps which can be taken. It looks at issues such as:

- adjusting to change
- retraining and education
- opportunities for work
- age discrimination
- working for yourself
- finances.

Complete with a range of personal accounts, this book is a first point of reference for those in mid-life keen to take control of their working lives again.

£9.99 0-86242-331-7

Managing Debt: A guide for older people
Edited by Yvonne Gallacher and Jim Gray

A significant proportion of older people continue to experience financial problems in retirement. This comprehensive book aims to help those people break free from the vicious debt cycle. It provides information, advice and guidance on managing debt. Topics covered in detail include:

- getting into debt
- negotiating with creditors
- money advice
- prioritising debts and dealing with emergencies
- bankruptcy
- understanding the law and your rights.

Written in clear, jargon free language, the book contains examples, sample letters, case studies and a glossary of terms, and is a complete self-help guide for people with financial problems.

£7.99 0-86242-236-1

Your Guide to Retirement
Ro Lyon
A comprehensive handbook for older people on the point of retirement, this book is full of practical information and advice

on all the opportunities available. It also points readers in the right direction to obtain more information when required. Drawing on Age Concern's wealth of experience, it covers everything you need to know, including:

- managing your money
- staying healthy
- making the most of your time
- housing options
- relationships

Your Guide to Retirement is easy to use and designed to encourage everyone to view retirement as an opportunity not to be missed. £7.99 0-86242-350-3

Health and care

CARERS HANDBOOK SERIES

This series has been written for the families and friends of older people. It guides readers through key care situations and aims to help readers make informed, practical decisions. All the books in the series:

- are packed full of detailed advice and information
- offer step-by-step guidance on the decisions which need to be taken
- examine all the options available
- include practical checklists and case studies
- point you towards specialist help
- help you to draft a personal plan of action
- are up to date with recent guidelines and issues
- draw on Age Concern's wealth of experience.

Caring for someone with cancer
Toni Battison
£6.99 0-86242-382-1

Caring for someone with a sight problem
Marina Lewycka
£6.99 0-86242-381-3

Caring for someone with a hearing loss
Marina Lewycka
£6.99 0-86242-380-5

Caring for someone with a heart problem
Toni Battison
£6.99 0-86242-371-6

Caring for someone with arthritis
Jim Pollard
£6.99 0-86242-373-2

Caring for someone with diabetes
Marina Lewycka
£6.99 0-86242-374-0

Caring for someone at a distance
Julie Spencer-Cingöz
£6.99 0-86242-367-8

Caring for someone with an alcohol problem
Mike Ward
£6.99 0-86242-372-4

Caring for someone who has had a stroke
Philip Coyne with Penny Mares
£6.99 0-86242-369-4

Choices for the carer of an elderly relative
Marina Lewycka
£6.99 0-86242-375-9

Caring for someone who is dying
Penny Mares
£6.99 0-86242-370-8

Caring for someone who has dementia
Jane Brotchie

£6.99 0-86242-368-6

The Carer's Handbook: what to do and who to turn to
Marina Lewycka

£6.99 0-86242-366-X

Caring for someone with depression
Toni Battison

£6.99   0-86242-347-4

Caring for someone with memory loss
Toni Battison

£6.99   0-86242-358-9

Bulk order discounts

Age Concern Books is pleased to offer a discount on orders totalling 50 or more copies of the same title. For details, please contact Age Concern Books on 0870 44 22 120. (Fax: 0870 44 22 034.)

Customised editions

Age Concern Books is pleased to offer a free 'customisation' service for anyone wishing to purchase 500 or more copies of the title. This gives you the option to have a unique front cover design featuring your organisation's logo and corporate colours, or adding your logo to the current cover design. You can also insert an additional four pages of text for a small additional fee. Existing clients include many of the biggest names in British industry, retailing and finance, the trades unions, educational establishments, the statutory and voluntary sectors, and welfare associations.

For full details, please contact Sue Henning, Age Concern Books, Astral House, 1268 London Road, London SW16 4ER. Fax: 020 8765 7211. Email: hennings@ace.org.uk

Visit our website at www.ageconcern.org.uk/shop

INDEX